The August Uprising,

The August Uprising, 1924

The Georgian Anti-Soviet Revolt and the Birth of Democratic Socialism

ERIC LEE

McFarland & Company, Inc., Publishers

Jefferson, North Carolina

ISBN (print) 978-1-4766-9866-3
ISBN (ebook) 978-1-4766-5656-4

Library of Congress cataloging data are available

Library of Congress Control Number 2025037114

Front cover image: *1924* by Levan Chogoshvili (courtesy of the artist).

Printed in the United States of America

McFarland & Company, Inc., Publishers
Box 611, Jefferson, North Carolina 28640
www.mcfarlandpub.com

For the Georgian people

Acknowledgments

I WANT TO THANK THE MANY INDIVIDUALS WITHOUT whom this book would not have been possible: Gio Akhvlediani, Natalia Alhazishvili, Timothy Blauvelt, Eric Chenoweth, George Curtin, Roger Darlington, Steve Davis, Brendan Jackson, Levan Jikia, Stephen Jones, Adrian Karatnycky, Irakli Khvadagiani, Beka Kobakhidze, Otar Kobakhidze, Martin Lee, Tristan Masat, Liam McNulty, John Medhurst, Peter Nasmyth, Roy Nitzberg, Marcel Röthig, Sarah Slye, Khatuna Tskhadadze, and Dato Turashvili.

In 2022, I spent a month in the Writers' House in Tbilisi as a writer-in-residence. This was a fantastic opportunity, and I want to particularly acknowledge the support of Natasha Lomouri, director of the Writers' House, who also shared with me the contents of the newly-opened Museum of the Repressed Writer there.

I wrote much of this book, as the previous ones, in the wonderful London Library. There is no better place in London to write.

I want to especially thank Giorgi Tchkadua, who worked as my research assistant in Tbilisi and provided considerable help with locating and translating Georgian and Russian texts.

Above all, thanks to Cindy Berman, who came with me on my first visit to Georgia in 2010 and has continued along for the ride ever since. Without her advice, help, patience, and love, this book and my previous ones would not have been written.

Contents

Contents

PART III—Socialism and Communism

Preface

IN 1924, AT A MEETING OF THE Soviet Communist leadership in Moscow, Stalin's trusted comrade Sergo Orjonikidze faced challenging questions.

He was accused of the excessive use of force in the suppression of a nationwide uprising in Georgia earlier in the year. Orjonikidze, like Stalin, was born in Georgia, and in 1924, he served as Moscow's imperial viceroy when the rebellion broke out. Orjonikidze panicked and ordered arrests, the taking of hostages, mass executions of prisoners, and more. Thousands of opponents of the new Communist regime were mowed down by machine gun fire, their bodies thrown into mass graves.

The world was paying attention, and the news could not have come at a worse time for a Soviet government eager to negotiate trade deals and diplomatic recognition with the West. Some Soviet Communist leaders felt that Orjonikidze had gone too far.

"We conducted mass shootings," he admitted. "Perhaps we overdid it slightly, but that can't be helped now."[1]

This book tells the story of the 1924 uprising in Georgia, a small country wedged between Russia and Turkey. For centuries, Georgia was subject to frequent invasions by its neighbors on all sides. By the beginning of the nineteenth century, it had come under Russian "protection," giving up its independence in exchange for a degree of safety. But as in the other border states in that empire, there was increasing support for the country's independence. The overthrow of the Romanov regime in March 1917 made that possible. Under the leadership of the Georgian Social Democrats, who were *democratic* Marxists, the country experienced nearly four years of freedom, including a multi-party system, free elections (with votes for women), and respect for human rights.

The most famous Marxist of the time, Karl Kautsky, who was an early critic of the Bolsheviks, visited Georgia for a few months. He wrote: "In comparison with the hell which Soviet Russia represents, Georgia appeared as a paradise."[2]

1

Georgia once again came under Russian rule in 1921 following a Red Army invasion. This led to peaceful protests and armed revolts, culminating in the national uprising that began in late August 1924.

That uprising, which was quickly and bloodily suppressed, would be just a footnote to history but for one thing: it provided the proverbial straw that broke the camel's back, leading to the final split between the world's Socialist and Communist parties.

It is not a familiar story to readers around the world, and not even in Georgia itself. Decades after the events described here, even Soviet historians pointed out that no full-length books had been published on the subject in the USSR. In the West, the 1924 uprising in Georgia was almost completely forgotten.

To understand how Socialism and Communism differed and how they grew into distinct movements that were often quite hostile to each other, we need to go back to the beginning and find key moments when the two movements diverged.

We have a rough idea of when this happened because in 1914, at the time of the outbreak of the First World War, all the Socialist, Social Democratic, and Labor parties belonged to the same broad movement known as the Second International. They included Lenin's Bolshevik party and the more moderate and democratic Mensheviks.

Yet a decade later, the rift between those parties, between the supporters of the Bolsheviks and their opponents, had grown so great that in Germany, for example, they were unable to unite even to stop Hitler and the Nazis. It may not be possible to specify when the "divorce" between the movements became final, but I think 1924 is a pretty good year for that, and this book explains why.

We will begin by briefly telling the story of Georgia's period of independence from 1918 to 1921. The Georgian Social Democrats had come to power and created a liberal democratic state, which stood in stark contrast to the emerging totalitarian regime being created by their Russian neighbors to the north.

That experiment—a society that respected human rights but also aimed to achieve greater social equality—was brought to a crashing end with the Red Army invasion of 1921, which Stalin ordered without the knowledge of Lenin or Trotsky (who was then commander of the Red Army).

But the Soviet conquest did not mean that Georgians happily accepted

Russian rule. The new regime, with its attacks on the trade unions, political parties, the Church, and even the co-operatives, remained deeply unpopular. Resistance was inevitable, and planning began for a nation-wide uprising, which finally began on August 28, 1924.

That rebellion, and the way it was suppressed, is a largely forgotten but important part of the story of the eventual split between the Socialists and Communists in nearly every country.

Not everyone was horrified at the behavior of the Soviets following the Georgian uprising. There were some on the Left who, due to their loyalty to the Bolshevik regime, acted as apologists for the Soviets and defended the bloody suppression of the 1924 revolt. They were part of a phenomenon that persisted throughout decades of totalitarian rule, which has been described as the "treason of the intellectuals."

Some prominent writers and thinkers believed that lying on behalf of a totalitarian state was the right thing to do. Hitler, Mussolini, and Stalin all had their supporters in democratic countries—supporters who could be counted on to defend the indefensible. That phenomenon has continued well into the twenty-first century, as some in the West justify Russian aggression against its neighbors, including Ukraine.

Following the crushing of the 1924 rebellion, leaders of the European Social Democratic and Labor parties asked Karl Kautsky, perhaps the most uncompromising critic of the Communists, to draft a resolution on the subject. As a result, for the first time, the Socialists acknowledged that they no longer had anything in common with the Communists. The split was now final.

And that split was due in no small part to the Georgian uprising of 1924.

A Note on Language

WHERE POSSIBLE, I USE THE TERM "Social Democratic" instead of "Menshevik" to describe the party that ruled Georgia during its years of independence (1918–1921). The label "Menshevik" was used by the Bolsheviks in a derogatory way, and it originally referred to a temporary minority at the 1903 congress of the Russian Social Democratic Labor Party. In any event, by 1924, the Russian Mensheviks and the Georgian Social Democrats were arguably no longer in the same party, as a rift had opened between them.

I have also used the terms "Social Democratic" and "Democratic Socialist" as synonyms. I know that some people think that there are huge differences between the two, but in terms of what this book discusses—the rift between the Socialist and Communist movements—the terms can be used interchangeably. I also use "Bolshevik" and "Communist" to mean the same thing. The party Lenin led was confusingly known for a time as the Russian Communist Party (Bolsheviks).

When referring to the Soviet secret police, I try to stick with the term "Cheka," which was the original name. Other names included GPU, OGPU, NKVD, MVD, and KGB. The term "Cheka" is widely understood to cover all the various Russian and Soviet secret police forces from 1917 onwards.

I also avoid references to the "October Revolution," as the Communists called the events in Petrograd in November 1917. Rather than a popular uprising, it was much more of a coup d'état, which is the term I use to describe it.

Finally, the Georgian capital was known as "Tiflis" until 1936, when the name was Georgianized to "Tbilisi." I use Tiflis to describe events there before 1936.

Timeline

1783: Georgia signs a treaty making it a Russian protectorate.

1801: Russia begins the annexation of Georgia.

1892: Georgia's first Marxist organization is formed.

1903: The Russian Social Democratic Labor Party splits into Bolshevik and Menshevik factions; the Georgian Social Democrats overwhelmingly side with the Mensheviks.

1905: Outbreak of a peasant rebellion in the western Georgian province of Guria. Revolution across the empire, including Georgia.

1906: Guria falls back under Russian control. Elections are held across the empire for the first State Duma. In Georgia, the Social Democrats win with large majorities.

1917: The Russian Revolution. The Tsar abdicates, while in Georgia, his Viceroy resigns, turning over the government to the Social Democratic Party. In a coup d'état in November, the Bolsheviks seize power in Russia. Elections are held for the Constituent Assembly across the country, including in Georgia. The Georgian Orthodox Church becomes independent of the Russian church.

1918: The Bolsheviks disperse the Constituent Assembly and set up their dictatorship. Georgia, Armenia, and Azerbaijan break off from Russia and briefly form a federation. On May 26, after that federation collapses, Georgia declares independence, with Social Democrat Noe Zhordania as its leader. Georgia and Ottoman Turkey sign a peace agreement as German troops enter the country. A brief war breaks out between Georgia and Armenia. Karl Kautsky publishes *The Dictatorship of the Proletariat*, a book-length attack on the Bolshevik regime from a Marxist perspective. Lenin writes a book in response, *The Proletarian Revolution and the Renegade Kautsky*. The Russian Civil War begins; independent Georgia adopts

5

a position of neutrality. Following the end of the First World War, German troops withdraw from Georgia and are replaced by the British.

1919: Elections to the Georgian Constituent Assembly: several parties compete, and the Social Democrats win a landslide victory. General Denikin's Volunteer Army engages in border clashes with the Georgians. There is rising tension between the British, who support Denikin, and the Georgians. On November 7, Georgian Communists make a failed coup attempt—the first of several.

1920: Russia and Georgia sign a peace treaty. In exchange for Russian recognition of their independence, the Georgians legalize the Communist Party. The British forces complete their withdrawal from Georgia. The other Transcaucasian republics, Armenia and Azerbaijan, fall under Soviet rule. In September, a delegation from the Second International, including Karl Kautsky and Ramsay MacDonald, arrives in Georgia.

1921: In February, the Russian army invades Georgia and, after several weeks of fighting, establishes Soviet rule, forcing the Georgian Republic's leaders into exile. Their last act is to adopt and publish the country's Constitution. Sporadic rebellions break out against Soviet rule, most notably in the province of Svaneti. In July, Stalin visits Tiflis for the first time in years and meets with a hostile reception. The Russian Civil War ends. In the naval fortress of Kronstadt just off the coast of St. Petersburg, sailors rebel against Soviet rule; their rebellion is quickly and violently suppressed. Following the failure of "War Communism," Lenin's New Economic Policy, with its liberalization measures, is introduced in Soviet Russia.

1922: Leaders of the three Internationals meet in Berlin in an attempt at reunification of the international Left. The meeting ends in failure, with the question of Georgia playing a surprisingly important role.

1923: Following the failure to find common ground with the Communists, the two Socialist Internationals merge to create the Labour and Socialist International (LSI). The Georgian Social Democratic Party, which had enjoyed a semi-legal existence in the country, is forced by the Soviets to dissolve. It continues its struggle underground. In Georgia, the military leadership of the underground is arrested and shot.

1924: Lenin dies. On August 28, a national uprising begins in Chiatura in western Georgia and is swiftly suppressed. The victorious Communist regime kills thousands. The British Labour Party and French Socialists fail to support Georgia despite earlier commitments to do so. The LSI Executive agrees for Karl Kautsky to write a resolution on the Soviet regime in the aftermath of the massacre in Georgia. The Georgian Social Democrats are among the first to use the term "red fascist" to describe the new regime in their country.

1925: Noe Zhordania publishes a short book analyzing the results of the failed 1924 uprising.

1951: Adoption of the Frankfurt Declaration—*Aims and Tasks of Democratic Socialism*—as the foundational document of the newly formed Socialist International. It repeats many of Karl Kautsky's formulations from decades earlier.

1991: On April 9, Georgia declares independence, reviving the national flag and anthem of the first Georgian republic. On May 26, the 73rd anniversary of Georgian independence, presidential elections are held.

PART I

Dictatorship and Democracy

CHAPTER 1

October and Its Critics

THE BOLSHEVIK COUP D'ÉTAT IN November 1917, led by Lenin and Trotsky, overthrew the Provisional Government and was immediately condemned by nearly all the other Russian Socialist factions, including the Mensheviks and Socialist Revolutionaries (SRs). A breakaway faction of the latter, the Left SRs, supported Lenin's regime for several months.

The descent of the Bolshevik regime into dictatorship was surprisingly swift. The newspapers of opposition political groups, including Socialist parties, were suppressed within a few weeks. The decision by the Bolsheviks on January 19, 1918, to shut down the Constituent Assembly—Russia's first democratically elected legislature—marked the end of the country's experiment with democracy. The feared Cheka, the secret police, was formed barely a month after the coup, and the first labor camps were established not long after.

This was not the regime Lenin promised in his 1917 pamphlet, *State and Revolution*, which anticipated a rapid "withering away of the state."

Among the first and most significant critics of the Bolsheviks was Lenin's old comrade, Julius Martov, the leader of the left-wing faction of the Mensheviks. Martov described the Bolshevik coup d'état as "an attempt to create a state machine very similar in its structure to the former military and bureaucratic type"—meaning the tsarist regime—but "in the hands of a small party."

The Soviet state, he wrote, "might be presented to the masses … as the destruction of the old state machinery, the birth of a stateless society based on a minimum of coercion and discipline."[1] But the opposite was taking place. The Bolsheviks were busy creating a highly coercive and powerful state that tolerated no dissent.

Menshevik concerns about Lenin's dictatorial tendencies preceded the coup d'état and indeed were at the root of the conflict between the two factions. The Mensheviks and other Socialists inside Russia became early critics of the Bolsheviks.

But outside of Russia, many Socialists were initially quite support-ive of Lenin and his party. Even Socialists who refused to join the newly created Communist parties, such as America's Eugene V. Debs, were early admirers of Lenin's regime. "From the crown of my head to the soles of my feet, I am Bolshevik, and proud of it," Debs wrote.[2]

A few early critics stand out. Among the best-known is Rosa Luxem-burg. Born in Poland in 1871, Luxemburg had been active in the German Social Democratic Party on its left wing for some time. A strong interna-tionalist, she spent most of the First World War in prison for her anti-war views.

She distrusted Lenin and, in 1904, wrote a powerful attack on his views regarding the party. The article was published in Lenin's newspaper, *Iskra*, and also in Karl Kautsky's *Die Neue Zeit*. As Bertram Wolfe wrote, Luxemburg "was offended in her whole being by Lenin's worship of cen-tralism, his implicit contempt for the working class … and his distrust of all spontaneous developments and of spontaneity itself."[3]

"We can conceive of no greater danger to the Russian party than Lenin's plan of organization. Nothing will more surely enslave a young labor movement to an intellectual elite hungry for power than this bureau-cratic strait jacket," Luxemburg wrote.[4] Where Lenin spoke of Socialists being "joined" to the working class, Luxemburg responded that "Social Democracy is not joined to the organization of the proletariat. It is itself the proletariat."[5]

Lenin's proposals triggered the split in the Russian Social Democratic Party between the centralizing, authoritarian Bolsheviks and the more moderate, democratic Mensheviks. Luxemburg predicted that Lenin's proposals would produce an all-powerful Central Committee. "The Cen-tral Committee," she wrote, "would be the only thinking element in the party. All other groupings would be its executive limbs."[6]

She summed up her views on Lenin and the Bolsheviks with these oft-quoted words: "Historically, the errors committed by a truly revolu-tionary movement are infinitely more fruitful than the infallibility of the cleverest Central Committee."[7]

The First World War brought with it the collapse of the Second Inter-national. Its leading parties, including the German Social Democrats, chose to support their governments. This betrayal of internationalist val-ues brought Luxemburg closer to Lenin.

When the Bolsheviks took power in Russia in November 1917,

Luxemburg took a position of critical support towards them. In some ways, her booklet, *The Russian Revolution*, is far more critical of the Mensheviks and Kautsky than of Lenin. She attacked the Menshevik leaders Pavel Axelrod and Fyodor Dan, who, she said, "wanted to collaborate at all costs with those classes and parties from which came the greatest threat of danger to the revolution and to its first conquest, democracy."[8]

Her booklet also contains criticisms of Lenin and the Bolsheviks but, in most cases, from a more left-wing perspective. For example, she opposed the Bolshevik support—on paper—for the self-determination of nations. Luxemburg had almost no sympathy for that idea, and the small Social Democratic party she had led in Poland stood *against* independence for that country. She described the "right of self-determination of nations," which the new Soviet regime had embraced, as "nothing but hollow, petty-bourgeois phraseology and humbug."[9]

But when it came to the Bolsheviks' suppression of democracy, particularly their dissolution of the elected Constituent Assembly, her old criticisms of Lenin surfaced again. "The remedy which Trotsky and Lenin have found, the elimination of democracy as such, is worse than the disease it is supposed to cure," she wrote.[10]

Luxemburg attacked several other Bolshevik policies, and her commitment to a bottom-up, grassroots revolution motivated that criticism. She believed strongly in spontaneity and rejected the top-down, vanguardist approach of the Bolsheviks.

She summed up the left critique of Bolshevism in this powerful passage: "Freedom only for the supporters of the government, only for the members of one party—however numerous they may be—is no freedom at all," she wrote. "Freedom is always and exclusively freedom for the one who thinks differently."[11]

In the end, despite her differences with the Bolsheviks, she helped to found the Communist Party of Germany. Luxemburg was murdered in January 1919 during the Spartacist uprising in Berlin. Had she lived, she might have remained a brave and independent voice, disagreeing at times with the Bolsheviks, or, perhaps like her friend Clara Zetkin, she might have eventually accepted party discipline and muted her criticism.

After her death, the Bolsheviks were quick to claim her legacy as their own. Even today, more than a century after her murder, there is an annual march in Berlin to honor her *and* Lenin—a march which ends at a cemetery in East Berlin, by the graves of several top German Stalinist functionaries.

Rosa Luxemburg never had the opportunity to visit Soviet Russia, but two years after the Bolshevik seizure of power, the 47-year-old British philosopher Bertrand Russell did so as part of a Labour Party delegation. Russell was already quite a prominent figure, giving him access not only to Soviet leaders (he had a one-on-one session with Lenin) but also considerable freedom to travel and meet ordinary people. He summarized what he learned in a book, *The Practice and Theory of Bolshevism*. Russell did not like what he saw. "I cannot enter into the conspiracy of concealment which many Western Socialists who have visited Russia consider necessary," he wrote.[12]

Here is how he described the "workers' state" founded by the Bolsheviks: "A sweated wage, long hours, industrial conscription, prohibition of strikes, prison for slackers, diminution of the already insufficient rations in factories where the production falls below what the authorities expect, an army of spies ready to report any tendency to political disaffection and to procure imprisonment for its promoters."

"This," he concluded, "is the reality of a system which still professes to govern in the name of the proletariat."[13] Russell expected things to get even worse (as they did). "This is what I believe to be likely to happen in Russia," he wrote. "The establishment of a bureaucratic aristocracy, concentrating power in its own hands, and creating a régime just as oppressive and cruel as that of capitalism."[14]

Indeed, it could be even more oppressive and cruel than capitalism. Despite what he saw in Russia, Russell supported the British Labour Party and the emerging idea of *democratic* socialism. "Russian Communism may fail and go under," he wrote, "but Socialism itself will not die."[15]

Not only Socialists criticized the new Bolshevik regime at that time. Some of the strongest left-wing critics came from the anarchist movement—the American Emma Goldman being one of the best-known. Like Bertrand Russell, Goldman spent time in Soviet Russia, following her expulsion from the United States.

"Two years of earnest study, investigation, and research convinced me that the great benefits brought to the Russian people by Bolshevism exist only on paper," she wrote. That paper was "painted in glowing colours to the masses of Europe and America by efficient Bolshevik propaganda. As advertising wizards, the Bolsheviks excel anything the world had ever known before. But in reality, the Russian people have gained nothing from the Bolshevik experiment."[16]

Another powerful voice against the Bolsheviks was the American Federation of Labor leader, Samuel Gompers. Though Gompers was not a supporter of the Socialist Party, he was one of the most influential figures in the international labor movement. He was also an early and implacable opponent of the Bolshevik dictatorship.

In 1921, the 71-year-old Gompers co-authored a book about Russia with William English Walling, a former Socialist Party leader who had visited Russia before the revolution and wrote two books about it. Walling broke with the Socialist Party during the First World War and found in Gompers an ally for his criticism of the new regime in Russia. The book was entitled *Out of Their Own Mouths: A Revelation and an Indictment of Sovietism* and it consisted mainly of Soviet documents translated into English. Gompers and Walling concluded: "There is no possible common ground between Bolshevism and organized labor."[17]

They were among the first to link their criticisms of the Bolshevik regime specifically to the recent invasion of Georgia and its subjugation to Soviet rule. They included an appendix entitled "The Turko-Bolshevik attack on the Labor Government of Georgia." Quoting from an appeal by the Georgian leaders to the international labor movement, Gompers and Walling wrote that "the whole Labor and Socialist press of Europe, both the moderates of the Right Wing and the orthodox Marxists and revolutionists of the Center, with few exceptions, has denounced this conquest as an example of the crudest imperialism. For example, *Die Freiheit* of Berlin, organ of the Independent Socialists, condemns the Soviet action against Georgia as a 'brutal imperialistic coup d'état.'"[18]

As we shall see in the course of this book, the Soviet invasion of independent Georgia in 1921 played a significant role in turning parts of the left and labor movement against the Russian Communist regime.

Some early left-wing critics of the Soviet regime are not as well-known as Martov, Luxemburg, Goldman, Russell, or Gompers. One of those was the French Esperantist Eugene Lanti, who founded the left-wing *Sennacieca Asocio Tutmonda* (SAT) in August 1921.[19]

A year after founding SAT, and disappointed to learn that the Communist International (Comintern) had decided not to adopt Esperanto as an official language, Lanti visited Soviet Russia for the first time. He was not happy with what he saw. In a series of articles, he criticized the Soviet system. "No political motive can force me to keep silent about the poor impressions I brought back from Russia," he wrote.[20]

As journalist Masha Karp wrote, "Thanks to his first-hand experience [in Russia], Lanti was one of the very few people among the Western left who, in the late 1920s, was fully aware of its disastrous consequences." Lanti shared his views with a young Englishman then living in Paris. He was the first to sow "the seeds of doubt about the success of the Russian Revolution in the young man's mind."[21]

That young man was Eric Blair, better known today as George Orwell.

CHAPTER 2

The Dictatorship
of the Proletariat

IN 1859, DECADES BEFORE THE BOLSHEVIK SEIZURE of power in Russia, Karl Marx explained why a Socialist revolution in that country was impossible. In this oft-cited passage from his book, *A Contribution to the Critique of Political Economy*, Marx wrote:

> At a certain stage of development, the material productive forces of society come into conflict with the existing relations of production.... From forms of development of the productive forces, these relations turn into their fetters. Then begins an era of social revolution.[1]

The "era of social revolution" that Socialists desired could only happen when capitalism had matured to the point where it stood in the way of further development. By 1917, Marxists around the world understood that while countries like the United States, Germany, or Britain may well have been ripe for Socialist revolution in the early twentieth century, Russia most certainly was not.

In the decades leading up to 1917, Karl Kautsky was the most influential Marxist writer in the world. His 1909 book, *The Road to Power*, summed up ideas shared by all Marxists at the time. In that book, he quoted an earlier article he wrote in 1904: "A revolution in Russia could not, for the present, establish a socialist regime. The country's economic conditions are too immature for that."[2] This argument was not controversial in 1904 or 1909. As Kautsky later pointed out, all of his critics in later years—and he specifically named Lenin, Trotsky, and Luxemburg—approved of his arguments in *The Road to Power*.

Kautsky was the leading theoretician of the German Social Democratic Party (SPD) and, by extension, of the Second International. He was the founding editor of *Die Neue Zeit*, the leading Socialist journal in the world, and the author of many of the most important books about

Marxism. To Russian Marxists, including Lenin, Kautsky was a mentor. His books were translated into Russian and were widely read—and among the Social Democrats, both Bolsheviks and Mensheviks counted themselves as his pupils.[3]

Kautsky was exceedingly interested in Russia. As an orthodox Marxist—perhaps the most orthodox Marxist of his time—Kautsky understood that for a country to undergo a Socialist revolution, it must first pass through a capitalist phase. In his writings, Kautsky emphasized the conditions necessary for socialism, including the maturity of the industrial working class (the proletariat). In an introduction to a reprinting of his *Road to Power* in 1920, he argued that Russia had met *none* of those criteria and the Bolsheviks had created a form of "barracks socialism."

Kautsky, like all Socialists, had enthusiastically welcomed the overthrow of the tsarist regime in Russia in February 1917. In *Die Neue Zeit*, Kautsky hailed the revolution for its destruction of the remnants of "feudalism," its creation of democratic institutions and freedoms, and its proclamation of a desire to immediately end the world war.[4] Kautsky called upon the German government to respond by offering generous peace terms. His plea was ignored. But his enthusiasm for what was happening in Russia declined precipitously when the Bolsheviks seized power in a coup d'état in November.

Karl Kautsky, 1926. The "Pope of Marxism," he was among the earliest critics of the Soviet regime (used by permission, AdsD der FES, 6/FOTA007108).

18

For many Socialists over the course of the twentieth century, we can precisely date their disappointment with the Soviet regime in Russia. For example, thousands quit the Communist Parties around the world in 1956 after the Red Army invaded Hungary. Others became disillusioned with Communism even earlier when Stalin signed his infamous pact with Hitler in 1939, triggering the Second World War. The Trotskyists broke from Stalin's regime even earlier than that.

Karl Kautsky didn't wait for the show trials of the 1930s, the *Holodomor* (terror famine) in Ukraine in 1932–33, or the invasion of Georgia in 1921. His opposition to Lenin and the Bolsheviks even pre-dated the dispersal of the Constituent Assembly in January 1918, the formation of the Cheka in December 1917, and the repressive measures targeting Russian Socialists who did not support the Bolshevik regime.

Kautsky published his first thoughts *just one week after the coup in Russia* for the left-wing *Leipziger Volkszeitung* in an article entitled "The Bolshevik Uprising." He considered the Russian economy too underdeveloped, with too small a working class, for a Socialist revolution. The country was not ready for this, and the result would not be good. Socialists, Kautsky wrote, should not rejoice at the Bolshevik seizure of power. Instead of a Socialist Utopia, the Bolshevik coup was more likely to bring on social and political chaos and to open the way for a counterrevolution that would overturn all the genuine achievements of the February Revolution.

We know that Kautsky was skeptical about Lenin's revolution from the very beginning not only because of his article for the *Leipziger Volkszeitung* but also because of a letter he received from the prominent Austrian Social Democrat Otto Bauer, written on November 24, a little more than two weeks after the Bolsheviks came to power.

Bauer had just been to Russia and told Kautsky of his concerns about the Bolsheviks being able to form a coalition with other Socialists and other issues. "I am not so pessimistic as you and still regard it as a real possibility that things will turn out well in the end," Bauer wrote.[5]

As it happened, things did not turn out well in the end, and Kautsky was one of the very few Socialists to grasp this from the outset. His doubts about the Bolsheviks grew steadily over the following months. By August 1918, Kautsky published an article in *Sozialistische Auslandpolitik* where he called on the Social Democrats to fight against Bolshevism.

Kautsky's articles from *Sozialistische Auslandpolitik* and *Leipziger*

Volkszeitung were now collected and published as a book, given the provocative title of *Die Diktatur des Proletariats (The Dictatorship of the Proletariat)*. It was the first book-length attack on the Soviet regime by a foreign Marxist.

And not just any Marxist—Kautsky was, after all, "the pope of Marxism." But at this point in his long career, Kautsky no longer wielded the authority he once commanded. During the First World War, which he opposed, Kautsky left the German Social Democratic Party (SPD), which had supported the war. He joined the Independent Social Democratic Party (USPD) instead. His platform for the previous few decades, *Die Neue Zeit*, had been taken away from him by the SPD leaders.

Otto Bauer. Austrian Socialist leader and critic of the Soviet invasion of Georgia (author's collection).

As a result, Kautsky's articles and book did not have the impact he might have been hoping for. Historian Moira Donald explained: "If Kautsky had produced such a critique in the pre-war years, the rest of the socialist world would have listened. But ... by 1917, the balance of influence had begun to change, and Kautsky's views no longer carried quite the same weight."[6]

The 63-year-old was no longer the unchallenged arbiter of Marxist orthodoxy— but he was not without influence. "He was still regarded," Donald continued, "as far too influential a figure to be ignored. That both Lenin and Trotsky, the leaders of the Bolshevik government, felt the need to devote precious time to writing and publishing refutations of Kautsky's views is adequate testimony both to the enduring importance of Kautsky himself, and to the extent to which his critique had stung the new government."[7]

As Dick Geary wrote, *The Dictatorship of the Proletariat* "became the gospel of those Marxists who rejected Bolshevik revolutionary practice" and it was the most comprehensive "defence of what might be described as the democratic Marxist position."[8]

Karl Kautsky's grandson John, a distinguished academic, summed up the significance of *The Dictatorship of the Proletariat* in these words:

> From the very beginning of the Bolshevik seizure of power in Russia, Karl Kautsky saw clearly and stated courageously that it was not and could not be a proletarian or a socialist, i.e., Western anticapitalist, revolution. And as the leading Marxist of his generation, he could authoritatively reject its claims to being Marxist as well. It is this message, delivered not as an impassioned plea to the emotions but as a calm and cool appeal to reason, that makes *The Dictatorship of the Proletariat* an important document in the history of Marxism and of the socialist movement and a milestone at the point of its path where communism and democratic socialism parted ways.[9]

It is said that when Lenin died in 1924, his library contained more books by Kautsky than by any other author, Russian or foreign, apart from his own work. As Moira Donald wrote, "for the leading Marxist theoretician of the time to reject so unambiguously, so categorically and so quickly the Bolshevik Revolution must have come as an unwelcome shock to the Bolshevik leadership."[10]

It certainly came as a shock to Lenin. According to one report, when Lenin read Kautsky's August 1918 piece from *Sozialistische Auslandpolitik*, he was "literally burning with anger." The Soviet leader, we learn, basically put everything else on hold to write a book-length answer to Kautsky, sitting up every day until late at night to do so.[11]

Despite Kautsky's increasing age and declining influence, Lenin and the Bolsheviks took his criticisms seriously. The title of Lenin's book, *The Proletarian Revolution and the Renegade Kautsky*, set the tone, which has been described as "bitter invective."[12]

John Kautsky wrote that Lenin

> insisted on his Marxian orthodoxy in the hope of winning over the European socialist parties ... to support his revolution. In order to do so he had to

destroy Kautsky's prestige as a Marxist. It was undoubtedly for this purpose, as well as to express his personal bitterness, that he employed an extremely abusive tone in his polemics with Kautsky.[13]

He cited several examples from Lenin's book to illustrate that tone: "a schoolmaster who has become as dry as dust," "tediously chews the cud," "twaddle," "this windbag," "a lackey of the bourgeoisie," and "extreme stupidity or very clumsy trickery." And that's only a sample. There is much more.[14]

Lenin lived for little more than six years after the Bolshevik seizure of power, and in all that time, he never wrote anything as long as his answer to Kautsky. The Soviet leader used the opportunity presented by Kautsky's attack to write what has been described as "the only serious attempt by Lenin to justify the Soviet regime in terms of Marxist theory."[15]

Kautsky's book was necessary in part because very few Marxists were prepared to challenge the Bolsheviks at that time. Rosa Luxemburg's book criticizing the Bolsheviks was published three years after her death. Kautsky challenged the Bolsheviks openly and immediately.

Kautsky published a response to Lenin in the summer of 1919 entitled *Terrorismus und Kommunismus (Terrorism and Communism)*. According to Moira Donald, this

> was a more direct assault on the Bolshevik regime, although the first two-thirds of the book are devoted to a general discussion of the nature of revolution, and a detailed historical analysis of the Paris Commune. If the early part was a typical example of Kautsky's scholasticism, the section on the Bolshevik regime was an uncharacteristically hard-hitting attack on the Bolshevik leadership. Whereas earlier Kautsky had stressed the difficulties under which the Bolsheviks were labouring—given their premature revolution—in *Terrorismus und Kommunismus*, he did not pull his punches.[16]

Here's how Donald summed up the significance of Kautsky's second book:

> This analysis published less than two years after the Bolsheviks came to power was a powerful indictment of the Bolshevik regime and a remarkably perceptive interpretation so early on, particularly as Kautsky had no first-hand knowledge of the situation in Russia. Kautsky's analysis of the new class society, the invention of the term state-capitalist, and his stress on the role of the bourgeoisie all anticipated future debates on the nature of Soviet society. These aspects of *Terrorismus und Kommunismus* were at least as important as Kautsky's forthright denunciation of the Bolsheviks' use of terror.[17]

Though Lenin was no longer available to write a response to Kautsky's second book, *Terrorism and Communism*, two senior Bolsheviks drafted book-length answers to Kautsky. The first was Leon Trotsky, then commander of the Red Army, which was fighting a bloody civil war against the various White armies. Trotsky explained how he wrote his book for a 1931 English edition—after his expulsion by Stalin from the Soviet Union:

> This book was written in 1920 in the car of a military train and amid the flames of civil war. This circumstance the reader must keep before his eyes if he wishes rightly to understand not only the basic material of the book, but also its harsh allusion, and particularly the tone in which it is written.[18]

That almost sounds apologetic, as if having become a victim of the new Stalinist regime himself, Trotsky in 1931 may have begun doubting his own certainty when he defended that regime in its infancy. He never reconciled with Kautsky, but he may have learned something from his bitter experience.

Trotsky gave his book the same title as Kautsky's—*Terrorism and Communism*—and it was published in 1920. As Donald pointed out, "The very fact that Trotsky devoted his time to writing this work at such a crucial period is indicative of the importance the Bolsheviks attached to Kautsky's criticism."[19]

"The tone of Trotsky's work is less vitriolic and less personal than that of Lenin," she wrote. "The book certainly does not lack strong criticism of Kautsky, but it is a more convincing defence of the Bolshevik revolution than Lenin's empty vituperations."[20]

Another somewhat lesser-known Bolshevik leader, Karl Radek, whom we shall meet later in this book, also penned a scathing rebuttal to Kautsky.[21]

Just as he had answered Lenin, Kautsky turned his attention to answering Trotsky. In 1921, he published *Von der Demokratie zur Staats-Sklaverei; eine Auseinandersetzung mit Trotzki (From democracy to state slavery; a confrontation with Trotsky)*.

During the final two decades of his life, Kautsky continued writing extensively about Soviet Russia from a critical, Marxist perspective.

As Dick Geary wrote regarding *The Dictatorship of the Proletariat*, "In the years between its publication and Kautsky's lonely death in Holland twenty years later, the former editor of *Die Neue Zeit* became obsessed with Lenin and his successors' 'betrayal' of Socialism, a theme developed in countless books and repetitious articles…. For an increasing number of Marxist intellectuals and revolutionaries, it was the German Social Democrat who had betrayed the heritage of Marx."[22]

But Kautsky was not betraying Marx. His view of Russia was articulated most clearly in 1909, and what he wrote then was the view of nearly all Marxists. In a 1920 preface to a new edition of *The Road to Power* Kautsky wrote about the new Bolshevik regime in Russia:

> In its beginnings syndicalist-anarchist (in practice, not in theory), it became, through the force of circumstances, a gigantic system of barracks socialism. No other kind of socialism is yet permitted by Russia's degree of development. I rejected the idea of a dictatorship of the minority as early as 1909. For Russia, I considered such a dictatorship possible, but not as a means for attaining to socialism, for which Russia is by no means ready.[23]

Kautsky's views on Russia were not popular in those first years after the Bolshevik coup. Many Socialists joined the newly formed Communist parties in their countries, and even many who remained inside the old Social Democratic parties were sympathetic to what Lenin and Trotsky were trying to achieve.

All that would begin to change, and Georgia, a small country on the fringe of the Russian empire, would play a surprisingly prominent role in that process. The visit of Socialist leaders to Georgia in 1920—Karl Kautsky among them—began to tip the balance against the Soviets.

Those Socialist leaders had discovered that another kind of revolution was possible.

CHAPTER 3

Another Revolution
Was Possible

IN 1956, FOLLOWING A WORKERS' UPRISING in Poznan, which threatened to topple the Polish Communist regime, a young academic at Warsaw University wrote an essay that he pinned to a campus bulletin board.

It was titled "What Is Socialism?" and it consisted, ironically, of a very long list of things socialism is *not*. The authorities quickly took it down, but it circulated underground for years. It was finally published in Poland after the fall of the Communist regime. The young academic was Leszek Kołakowski, who became one of the twentieth century's greatest philosophers and the author of the three-volume *Main Currents of Marxism*.

Socialism, Kołakowski wrote, is not "a society in which someone who has committed no crime sits at home waiting for the police." Nor is it "a society in which some people are unhappy because they say what they think, and others are unhappy because they do not." It is not "a state where people are compelled to lie." And so on. It's a very long list. In the end, he wrote: "Here is what socialism is: Socialism is a system that…. But what's the point of going into all these details? It's very simple: socialism is just a really wonderful thing."[1]

What strikes me now about Kołakowski's essay is precisely how easy it was to say what socialism should not be—and how hard it was to explain what it might be instead. The democratic socialism that Kołakowski embraced at that time lacked historical models. Many dictatorial regimes called themselves Socialist, including the one in Poland. But where were the positive models? The "wonderful thing" that socialism could have been?

This had long been a problem for the Left, especially after the Bolshevik seizure of power in 1917. Lenin and his comrades claimed to have created the first Socialist country. But for critics of the Bolsheviks, if this was socialism, it was not worth fighting for—indeed, it was worth fighting against.

In 1920, some of Europe's leading Socialists found themselves visiting a country ruled by a Socialist party where people were not compelled to lie, and innocent citizens did not wait at home for the police.

They were members of parties affiliated to the Second International, which had collapsed during the First World War and was now reviving itself. That International held a congress in Geneva in 1920, and among the parties that sent representatives was the Georgian Social Democratic Party. Its six-member delegation included Irakli Tsereteli, a former minister in the Russian Provisional Government. Tsereteli was quite well-known among European Socialists from their pre-war congresses.

After Georgia declared its independence on May 26, 1918, its government worked hard to win recognition from the great powers. These included Britain, France, Italy, and the United States. But they were also keen to win the support of the Social Democratic and Labor parties affiliated with the Second International. Tsereteli invited representatives of the relaunched Second International to visit Georgia.

The Georgian Social Democrats felt they had something worth sharing. In the years leading up to 1917, they had been members of the Russian Social Democratic Party and opponents of Georgian separatism. They hoped that a future Russian Revolution would bring an end to the empire, to be replaced by a federation, including an autonomous Georgia. But the Bolshevik coup d'état forced them to rethink their position. They did not want to live under Communist rule and opted for independence from Russia.

The society they created was an experiment in democratic socialism—with powerful trade unions and cooperatives, a radical land reform policy, and full political rights for all, including votes for women. In free elections, the Georgian Social Democrats won a large majority, though rival political parties competed freely for power. Georgia, under Social Democratic rule, was everything Soviet Russia was not.

The delegation included some of the most prominent politicians of the time. James Ramsay MacDonald was a leader of the British Labour Party, though he was no longer a Member of Parliament, having lost his seat in the 1918 elections. MacDonald would soon return to Parliament, and less than four years later, he led Britain's first Labour government. Tom Shaw was a Labour MP from Preston, Lancashire. Ethel Snowden was the only woman on the trip in her own right. Like MacDonald and Shaw, she was a leader of the Labour Party and served on its National Executive

Members of the international Socialist delegation visiting Georgia in 1920 (author's collection).

Committee. In early 1920, she visited Russia. She was not pleased with what she saw and published a highly critical book, *Through Bolshevik Russia*.

The French members of the delegation to Georgia included Pierre Renaudel, Adrien Marquet, and Alfred Inghels. The Belgian delegation consisted of Emile Vandervelde and his wife Lalla, Louis de Brouckère, and Camille Huysmans, accompanied by his wife Marthe and daughter Sara, who acted as secretary to the delegation. Huysmans became the Belgian prime minister following the Second World War. Vandervelde, who had served as a minister in the government during the First World War, was president of the Labour and Socialist International until he died in 1938.

The best-known member of the delegation was Karl Kautsky, whose hostility towards the Bolsheviks was already quite well known.

After a long journey across Europe, they finally arrived in Tiflis. "It seemed very odd," wrote MacDonald. "There we were, having left for some days all that seemed to be of the West, having gone through the Bazaar and the mosques of Constantinople and proceeded far beyond towards the rising sun, and, at our journey's end, at last, we were being received by a President of the Republic of Georgia in a waiting room at the Tiflis railway station, covered with the most glorious Oriental rugs, but hung with the portraits of Karl Marx and his best-known disciples."[2]

They soon met with the Social Democratic Party's Central Committee. Snowden remembered that the delegation's "first business in Tiflis was to attend the special session of Parliament called in our honour, to hear a speech of welcome from each of the eight political parties represented in that Parliament."[3]

MacDonald described later visiting "the heart of the Caucasian mountains, surrounded by the wildest and the gayest rout of untamed mountaineers armed with sword, shield, and rifle" and then standing reverently "whilst an old priest by the light of altar candles guttering in the wind read to us an address of welcome which ended with 'Long live the International.'"[4]

A number of the visiting Socialists commented on how the local nobility had accepted the Social Democratic reforms. Sara Huysmans wrote that "large landowners had been disinherited with little difficulty." Ethel Snowden "met landlords who submitted cheerfully to the new system and noble ladies who rejoiced in their new-found economic liberties.."[5] "I met Princes who gloried in their new-found civic equality," recalled Ramsay MacDonald.[6]

They found none of the bitter class warfare that had torn Russia apart in the years following the Bolshevik coup in 1917. Unlike Russia, Georgia, experienced no civil war.

Ethel Snowden was interviewed by *The Times* on her return to London. She gave an entirely positive account of her visit. The Georgian people, she said, are "full of hope and determination. They have set up what is the most perfect Socialism in Europe."[7]

As *The Times* had earlier reported, Snowden was on the delegation to compare her experiences in Soviet Russia with Georgia: "I was immediately struck by the difference between the appearance of the people in Georgia and in Russia," she said. "The constant sight of misery in Russia was intolerable. The Georgians were in a physical condition infinitely superior to the Russians. They looked well-fed and well-clothed and, above all, genuinely happy. There was no terror in their faces. There were no demonstrations arranged by military order."[8]

Ramsay MacDonald, too, was interviewed by the *Manchester*

Guardian upon his return to England.[9] As the newspaper summarized the interview, the Labour leader described "a happy country under a Socialistic regime."

MacDonald told the journalist that he was "delighted with his visit to Georgia. It is, he said, a beautiful country and small as it is—its population is about four million—he believes it to have a great future. The Georgian Republic, as he reminded me, is Socialist, and, as a member of the Government had said to him, the aim of the Government is to organise it on I.L.P. lines." The I.L.P. was the Independent Labour Party, which MacDonald led.

Ramsay MacDonald. First Labour Prime Minister of Britain; visited Georgia in 1920 (author's collection).

MacDonald told the journalist about the Georgian land reform. This initiative, led by Noe Khomeriki, the agriculture minister, was an enormous success. While Soviet Russia struggled with the problem for years, trying a series of wildly different approaches, including sending out armed detachments from the cities to seize food from farmers, the result was often starvation in the cities and civil war in the countryside.

Not so in Georgia. MacDonald also noted that "the Georgians are intensely anti–Bolshevik and also anti–Russian, but there is active Bolshevik propaganda, which is not interfered with, as there is complete liberty of opinion."[10]

The "active Bolshevik propaganda" that MacDonald witnessed was a relatively new feature on the Georgian political scene. As the Communists had spent the first couple of years of Georgian independence trying to stage violent uprisings against the democratically elected government of the country, they were excluded from its political life. But following the May 1920 peace treaty between Soviet Russia and Georgia, the Communists were allowed to resume their legal activity—while continuing to maintain secret organizations that plotted the overthrow of the Social Democratic government.

Karl Kautsky arrived somewhat later than the others and stayed on for several months. He wrote a short book about Georgia, published in English as *Georgia, a Social-Democratic Peasant Republic: Impressions and Observations*. Kautsky was not uncritical of the Georgian Social Democrats, but his book summed up all their achievements, including the land reform, a strong trade union movement, and the growth of cooperatives.

Kautsky had his criticisms of the Georgian government. But in his summing up, Kautsky could not have been clearer. "In comparison with the hell which Soviet Russia represents," he wrote, "Georgia appeared as a paradise."[11]

The Second International and the Social Democratic and Labor parties it united represented, in the view of the Georgian Social Democrats, a world power no less important than Italy or Belgium. This was not a view shared by all, and some Georgians felt that their country's leaders were wasting time with Socialist politicians who had no real power.

But Trotsky took the international Socialist delegation to Georgia so seriously that he wrote an entire book about it. It was published in English as *Between Red and White* and it was his answer to the book Kautsky wrote after leaving Georgia.

If Noe Zhordania, the leader of the Georgian Social Democrats, and his comrades suffered from the illusion that the leading politicians of the Second International mattered, they were not alone, as the Soviet leadership shared the same fantasy. But as it turned out, neither the Second International nor the Allied Powers could do much for Georgia when Soviet Russia decided it was time to end Georgia's experiment in democratic socialism.

CHAPTER 4

The Experiment Ends

By May 1920, it had become clear to Lenin and other Soviet leaders that the tiny Georgian Bolshevik party would not overthrow the Social Democratic government in that country. Its attempts to do so had produced only farcical results. The party had almost no support in the small urban working class and none among the peasants.

If "Soviet Georgia" was ever to become a reality, a different strategy would have to be found. The Russians agreed to a peace treaty recognizing Georgian independence. The Georgians agreed to the legalization of the previously outlawed Communist Party and the release of jailed Party members. That explained why Ramsay MacDonald was able to witness open Bolshevik propaganda in the country.

The Georgian Communist Party had been banned, and some of its members jailed not because their ideas were unpalatable but because they rejected the rules underpinning the Georgian democracy. The Georgian Communists attempted repeated armed uprisings rather than participation in free elections. Under the terms of the new treaty, they promised to stop doing that.

The local Communist Party chose to focus on armed uprisings as a road to power rather than participation in free elections. Vera Broido described the situation in Georgia: "The new country was beset on all sides by hostile forces, but its worst enemy proved to be within: Georgian Bolsheviks recognised only one fatherland and one government and that was Lenin's Russia," she wrote. "These Bolsheviks fomented discontent and rebellion among disbanded soldiers and other unstable elements. In November 1919 they staged an abortive coup, after which almost a thousand of them were imprisoned by the Georgian government. Like their Russian counterparts, the Georgian Mensheviks had scruples about using violence against their opponents; they did not shoot the prisoners."[1]

The May 1920 treaty between Soviet Russia and Georgia was worthless. It was just a tactical move by the Soviets, as no one in Moscow had abandoned the project of bringing Georgia back under Russian rule. And no one in the Soviet leadership understood this better than the two Georgians, Stalin and Orjonikidze. They devised a new strategy, which mixed subversion with an eventual armed intervention by the Workers' and Peasants' Red Army.

In early February 1921, the time was ripe. Lenin was ill and inactive. Red Army commander Trotsky was out on an inspection tour of the Urals. It was time for Stalin and Orjonikidze to strike.

At first, several Georgian military detachments were disarmed by rebels in the Lori district and Shulavery, south of Tiflis near the Armenian border. The rebels called upon the peasants to rise up and oust the Menshevik rulers. The next day, the Georgian army reported that "regular units made a surprise attack upon our advanced posts" from Armenia, which was now under Soviet rule.

The controversy over whether this was a genuine civil war or brazen Soviet aggression had already begun. On Sunday, February 13, the Georgian Social Democratic newspaper *Borba* reported a full-scale revolt in the Lori-Borchalo area had broken out. It claimed that the revolt had been provoked by a foreign power.

It turned out that Stalin and Orjonikidze, who ran the revolutionary military committee for the Caucasus, had told the Politburo in Moscow that a popular revolution had broken out in Georgia. Its success was inevitable, they said. The help of the Red Army was needed only to ensure that the process was as brief and painless as possible. The Russian Communist leaders, Lenin included, trusted Stalin's judgment. After all, he was a Georgian himself.

However, Lenin remained somewhat concerned and issued orders that the Russian invaders behave with respect towards the Georgians, even towards Zhordania, and try to win their support. His orders were ignored as the Red Army faced increasingly stiff opposition—and as it became clear that no popular uprising was taking place in the country. Stalin and Ordjonikidze had made that part up.

A few days after the revolt had started, a "revolutionary committee" was set up by the rebels in Shulavery. It appealed to the Russian Soviet regime to help liberate Georgia from Menshevik rule. The rebels in the border area had been given a few days to establish the fact of a bona fide rebellion. Once that had happened, the Russians dropped all pretense and poured troops into Georgia from all sides.

Armenia had ostensibly been one of the causes of the fighting. Traditional Armenian-Georgian hostility had led to a perfectly "normal" border war. The Russians claimed to be intervening precisely to put an end to this sort of unending friction—or so Soviet historians were later to depict these events. Yet the departure of Soviet troops from Armenia, marching towards Tiflis, triggered a violent popular uprising in Georgia's neighbor.

Soviet rule in Armenia was crumbling. On February 16, newspapers in the Armenian capital of Yerevan reported some slight trouble. By evening, gunfire could be heard in the streets. Soviet Armenia collapsed overnight. The following day, there was more pressure on the Soviets as Haidar Bammat, the leader of a group of North Caucasian and Azerbaijani exiles living in Georgia, called upon the Georgian government to mobilize his people as allies. Given time, the Georgians, Armenians, and Azerbaijanis might have been able to pull it off. But they were not given time.

This would be significant for the planners of the 1924 uprising. With the support of the Armenians and Georgia's other neighbors, the Russians could be held off. Without that support, each of the Transcaucasian republics fell easily to the Soviet armies.

To the government in London, Georgia must have seemed to be a lost cause. Even though the British government had grown increasingly sympathetic to the Georgians, finally giving them the diplomatic recognition they had so long craved, providing practical military assistance at so late a stage was not in the cards. By early 1921, the British and the other Allies had accepted military defeat at the hands of the Red Army, having lost the Russian Civil War.

Meanwhile, French warships in the Black Sea shelled columns of Russian forces, which were now heading south, down the Georgian coast. Of all the Allied powers, only France offered actual military help during the war, and its shelling was the only concrete military aid Georgia received.

This, too, provided a lesson for the Georgian government-in-exile in 1924: foreign military support was critical to the success of an uprising against Communist rule.

At 9:00 on the evening of February 24, two weeks after the beginning of the Soviet assault (the "border incident" at Borchalo), the Georgian Government finally evacuated its capital. The fall of Tiflis was now imminent. Just before leaving Tiflis, the Georgian government sent a hasty telegram to Lenin and Trotsky in Moscow, pleading with them to call off the attack (even though the official line of the Soviet Government was that it had nothing to do with this).

Orjonikidze cabled Moscow: "The red banner is aloft" in Tiflis, he wrote. Friday, February 25, was declared the day of the triumph of the Georgian Soviet revolution and was celebrated as such for decades thereafter.

The Georgian Government and its army were heading for the coast, for the port city of Batumi which was already threatened from the north by the advancing Ninth Red Army and now from the south by the Turks.

In early March, the Soviet-backed "Revolutionary Committee," which now ruled most of the country, called on the Georgian Government to cease all military operations, recognize the new regime, and form a coalition government. To press the Social Democrats to accept this peace offer, the local Bolsheviks in Batumi organized an uprising against the government.

The Georgian Government now presided over a much smaller army than had existed just a few days earlier. Under these circumstances, the Georgian Government agreed on March 11 to open negotiations with the Soviets now in power in Tiflis. On Wednesday, March 16, at its final session in Batumi, the Georgian Constituent Assembly ordered the Government to withdraw from the country to continue the struggle from abroad.

The Soviet invasion and occupation of Georgia in 1921 provided a template for future invasions and occupations. Moscow's treaty with the Georgian Republic, signed in 1920, was designed to buy time before the Red Army could invade. The Soviet regime had no intention of allowing an independent and democratic socialist Georgia to thrive on its southern border.

When the invasion took place, the attempt to deny that Georgia was being invaded was also to be used as a template on other occasions when the Soviets wanted their aggression to appear more benign. In later years, Soviet invasions of Eastern European satellite states were justified with the claim that the Red Army had been invited to enter the country to save it from some awful fate.

Take the example of Hungary in 1956. According to a pro–Soviet account published in 1969, Hungarian Communists, following their overthrow by a popular revolution, "decided to use fraternal internationalist assistance to ensure victory in the armed struggle" against the new government. The Communist leadership in Budapest "addressed itself to the Soviet command requesting help for our people." And by "help," they meant armed intervention. "The government of the Soviet Union responded to the Hungarian request. Its troops crushed the armed counter-revolutionary centres."[2]

The Soviets continued with this line for many more years, right up until the December 1979 invasion of Afghanistan—again, at the "invitation" of a local, pro–Soviet government (whose leader, Hafizullah Amin, was murdered by the Soviet forces ten days after he invited them in). Even the post–Soviet Russians have adopted a version of this approach in their attempts to justify the 2022 invasion of Ukraine. They claim to have invaded Ukraine to save it, particularly the Russian-speaking eastern part of the country, from "neo–Nazis" who had seized power in Kyiv.

This justification for a brazen violation of a country's sovereignty is taken directly from the example of the 1921 Soviet invasion of Georgia at the invitation of a non-existent revolutionary government. As we shall see, the Soviet myth about a "workers' revolution" in Georgia that welcomed the assistance of the Red Army was discarded within a year of the invasion itself.

Only two weeks had passed from the border incident with Armenia to the panicked retreat from Tiflis. Three weeks more, and the Georgian independent republic had ceased to exist. For many years after that, Georgian exiles debated what had gone wrong and who was responsible.

One of the problems was the lack of solidarity between the three Transcaucasian countries in the years leading up to the 1921 invasion. Even the Armenian rebellion against Bolshevik rule, which occurred during the attack on Georgia, was not coordinated with the Georgians. This lesson was quickly learned by the exiled Georgian, Armenian, and Azerbaijani politicians. On June 10, 1921, less than three months after Georgia had fallen to Soviet rule, a joint declaration was issued by representatives of the exiled governments, including the North Caucasus region. It declared a military and economic union and was sent to all the great powers and the League of Nations. But it came too late to have any effect on the ground.

One of the most striking errors committed by the Georgian leaders was their naïve belief that the Allied powers, which had just recognized Georgia, would come to its aid. Once the British forces had withdrawn from Batumi in 1920, it was unlikely they or anyone else would return. The Great Powers, which Georgia counted on for support, were exhausted after years of war. Following the defeat of the White armies in Russia, they had little appetite to continue the armed struggle against the Bolsheviks.

Meanwhile, there was the impotence of the newly formed League of Nations, which would not become apparent until the 1930s. One might argue that the experience of democratic Georgia foreshadowed what would later happen to countries like Ethiopia and Spain, which fell victim to fascist aggression with the League of Nations being unable to help.

Equally naïve, perhaps more so, were the repeated appeals and protests made by the Georgian government to a regime in Moscow which, while hurling whole armies at Georgia, consistently denied any involvement in the war. While it may have been the case that Trotsky was unaware that the invasion had taken place, and Lenin seemed unaware of the genuine facts on the ground, the Georgian Social Democrats were never going to find a sympathetic ear in Moscow. Stalin and Orjonikidze were determined to end Zhordania and his comrades' rule in Tiflis.

The collapse of the democratic Georgian republic, its complete military defeat, seemed to bring an end once and for all to the dream of independence. But this was not to be the case. There was still one more battle coming.

CHAPTER 5

Stalin in Tiflis

IT SHOULD HAVE BEEN A TRIUMPHANT RETURN.

Born in the small Georgian city of Gori forty-three years earlier, Joseph Stalin spent his formative years as a revolutionary in Tiflis, Batumi, and Baku. But after the 1917 revolution that allowed him to come back from years of Siberian exile, he did not return to his family home. Instead, he went straight to Petrograd, taking up a leadership role in Lenin's Bolshevik party. With the Bolshevik seizure of power later that year, he was named a member of the *Sovnarkom*—the Council of People's Commissars.

Following the February 1921 Red Army invasion of Georgia, Stalin would now return to the country of his birth as the head of a triumphant military and political force.

Orjonikidze had cabled him just a few months earlier that the red flag was now flying over Tiflis. Stalin could come and see that for himself. As Robert Tucker wrote:

> Stalin arrived in Tiflis at the end of June 1921 to take part in an important plenary meeting of the *Kavburo*,[1] with local leaders in attendance, to consider policy questions affecting Georgia and Transcaucasia as a whole. His first visit in many years to his native land proved a very different experience from the return to Baku eight months before.[2]

Things did not go according to plan. At one point, Stalin agreed to speak to a mass meeting of railway workers, with a crowd estimated at 5,000. Though Stalin was not yet the undisputed leader of the Soviet state, he was part of the tiny group trusted by Lenin to lead the country. And though not yet the subject of adulation—the infamous "cult of personality" would come later—he was used to being accorded the respect owed to a People's Commissar.

Surrounded by armed agents of the Cheka, he began by congratulating the workers on overthrowing the Menshevik yoke. Tucker described what happened next:

His appearance on the speaker's platform was met with hisses, and old women in the audience shouted epithets like "Accursed one," "Renegade," and "Traitor." Isidore Ramishvili and Alexander Dgebuadze, two veteran Menshevik revolutionaries present in the audience, received an ovation, and the latter said to Stalin: "Why have you destroyed Georgia? What have you to offer by way of atonement?"[3]

Members of the audience were shouting, "Lies! There was no Menshevik yoke here! There was no Communist revolution in Georgia! Your troops have removed our freedom!"

Tucker added: "According to a present-day Soviet historian's account, Ramishvili was carried up to the platform by some of those present, and the crowd would not let Stalin speak."[4]

"Surrounded by the angry faces of his old comrades Stalin turned pale and could only stutter a few words of self-justification, after which he left the hall cowering behind his Russian bodyguard," wrote David Lang.[5]

The day after the disastrous meeting with the railway workers, a furious Stalin stormed into the Communist Party headquarters in Tiflis. Stalin attacked "local chauvinism" among the Communists and declared that the most urgent task of the Communist Party in his homeland was a ruthless struggle against the remnants of nationalism. Stalin was on the warpath, demanding that the local Communist party purge its ranks of patriots and "all who would not subordinate Georgia's interests to those of the entire Soviet Union."[6]

Lang noted that "such language, with its unmistakable overtones of new-born Great Russian imperialism, created a deplorable impression when coming from the lips of a native-born Georgian veteran of the liberation movement."[7]

Stalin was infuriated at the fact that the Social Democrats still seemed to be around and had not been crushed. He demanded a stricter policy and an end to the leniency that Lenin had advocated a few months earlier. Though he was not the all-powerful General Secretary that he would become later in the decade, Stalin still had some strings he could pull. He removed the veteran Bolshevik revolutionary Makharadze from his leadership role as chairman of the Georgian Revolutionary Committee. Instead, he was given the post of People's Commissar for Agriculture, a clear demotion.

To replace Makharadze, Stalin brought in another Georgian Bolshevik he thought he could trust to run the local Soviet government—Budu Mdivani. But as we shall see, Mdivani was even less likely to fight against Georgian nationalism than his predecessor.

Stalin was furious and held his old comrade, Filipp Makharadze, responsible.

Later that year, Makharadze made clear his doubts about the new regime he led in Tiflis. In a report to the Central Committee of the Russian Communist Party in Moscow, Makharadze wrote:

> The arrival of the Red Army and the establishment of Soviet power in Georgia had the outward appearance of a foreign occupation because in the country itself there was nobody who was ready to take part in a rebellion or a revolution.

One might counter that it *looked like* a foreign occupation because it *was* a foreign occupation.

Makharadze continued:

> And at the time of the proclamation of the Soviet regime there was, in the whole of Georgia, not even a single member of the party capable of organizing action or providing leadership and this task had been accomplished mainly by doubtful or sometimes even criminal elements.[8]

But it was not all about threats and demotions. Stalin knew how to apply a carrot-and-stick approach when dealing with the Georgian Communists. As Tucker wrote:

> He announced some benefits: Moscow would issue a loan of over six million gold roubles to the three Transcaucasian republics, and Azerbaijan would provide some oil products gratis to Georgia and Armenia.[9]

On July 6, Stalin appeared before what has been described as "a more docile audience"—the Tiflis Communist Party. He delivered an address "on the tasks of Communism in Georgia and the Transcaucasia." This time, no one hissed, and no one heckled him.

The heart of Stalin's speech, wrote Tucker, was a stern lecture to the Georgians on the necessity to "stamp out the hydra of nationalism." Returning to Tiflis after a lapse of years, Stalin said, he was unpleasantly struck by the lack of the solidarity that had existed in 1905–17 between workers of the different Transcaucasian nationalities, and that nationalism had developed among the workers and peasants. Three years of life under nationalist governments had left their mark. So, the Georgian Communists were faced with the task of carrying on a "ruthless struggle against nationalism"—indeed, of "burning out" the remnants of nationalism "with a red-hot iron."[10] We shall see that "red-hot iron" in action in the following chapters.

When Stalin returned to Tiflis in 1921, he was not greeted as a hero. Those who knew him and remembered him from his days in Georgia had their doubts about him—doubts that went back two decades or more.

Stalin was born in 1878 in Gori, a town west of Tiflis. His family was poor, and his prospects for life seemed bleak until his mother arranged for the young man to study to be a priest. That would have been his ticket to a better life outside of Gori. He attended the Tiflis Theological Seminary, where instead of becoming a priest, he was—like many others before him—radicalized. He read banned literature, including the writings of Karl Kautsky, and he became a Marxist.

Ronald Suny described what happened next:

> Sometime in late 1898, at the beginning of his last year at the seminary, Soso [Stalin] decided to visit Zhordania in his editorial offices…. According to a noteworthy memory by Zhordania, the young seminarian told the veteran of Georgian Marxism that he was "a dedicated reader of your journal and your articles. They have had a great effect on me. I have decided to give up the seminary and carry these ideas into the workers' midst. Give me advice." Since good propagandists were scarce, Zhordania was pleased by Jugashvili's intention but decided to test the young man's intellectual breadth. After a few questions on history, sociology, and political economy, it became clear that Soso had a very superficial understanding based largely on articles from kvali and Karl Kautsky's *The Erfurt Program*. Zhordania advised the seminarian to stay in school for another year and to take up self-education. "I will think about it," said Soso, and he left…. Reluctantly the new recruit to Marxism returned to the seminary, but the condescension that the older, more genteel intelligent displayed toward the youthful enthusiast did not long deter him.[11]

Five years later, the Russian Social Democratic Party split into Bolshevik and Menshevik factions. Georgian members of the Party, led by Noe Zhordania, took the side of the Mensheviks. Stalin, already estranged from Zhordania, embraced Lenin, who became his mentor and hero. There were very few Georgian Bolsheviks then or later. From the beginning, Stalin's comrades in Georgia began to doubt the young man, and it was not only his "superficial understanding" of Marxism that was an issue. Stalin behaved differently than other Socialists and seemed to lack the moral compass essential to membership in a revolutionary organization.

A story made the rounds that following his expulsion from the seminary, Stalin betrayed the names of others who shared his radical views. When confronted with the charge, Stalin allegedly defended himself, saying that the expulsion of the others from the seminary added to the ranks of revolutionaries and was a good thing.

Many other accusations followed, some appearing in memoirs by Stalin's Socialist comrades in the 1920s and later. For example, he was accused of betraying to the police the secret hiding place of the noted Armenian Bolshevik Stepan Shaumian, which only he knew.

While most biographers dismiss the idea that Stalin collaborated with the tsarist police, several authors make a compelling case—if circumstantial—that the Georgian's relationship with the Okhrana was more complicated than it might appear. Edward Ellis Smith's detailed study, *The Young Stalin: The Early Years of an Elusive Revolutionary* (1967), offers the strongest case that Stalin's life underground points to an ongoing relationship with the police.

The high point of interest in Stalin's relationship with the tsarist police came in 1956 when *Life* magazine in the United States published two articles linking the Soviet leader to the Okhrana.

The first was by former NKVD General Alexander Orlov, who had defected to the West nearly two decades earlier. Orlov claimed to have heard a detailed account of "Stalin's secret file" from a cousin of his and blamed the purge trials of the 1930s and especially Stalin's conflict with the top military leadership on the discovery of that file.

But more important was the publication of a letter in that same issue of *Life* that seemed to offer documentary proof that Stalin was an agent of the tsarist police. The letter was dated July 12, 1913, and was signed by Colonel Alexander Eremin, head of the Special Section of the Department of Police. Writing from the police headquarters in St. Petersburg, Eremin informed a captain in the distant Siberian town of Yeniseisk that one of the revolutionaries who had just been deported to his jurisdiction was, in fact, a former police collaborator. The agent's name was Josef Vissarionovich Jugashvili—who had only recently taken on the pseudonym "Stalin."

According to the Eremin letter, Stalin began giving information to the police following his 1906 arrest in Tiflis and continued working for them in Baku and then again in St. Petersburg. When the letter was written, Stalin had broken from the police following his election to the Bolshevik Central Committee.

The problem with Eremin's letter is that no one knows if it is genuine. The letter first surfaced in the 1930s, and there is reason to believe that Trotsky saw it or knew of its existence. But Trotsky chose to reject the view—then widely held—that Stalin had probably been a double agent. In the mid–1940s, the letter surfaced again in New York, having been passed around among White Russian emigres.

Its final publication in *Life* magazine was followed by a book-length treatment by journalist Isaac Don Levine, *Stalin's Great Secret*. Levine had authored the first English language biography of Stalin a quarter century earlier and considered the letter genuine.[12] Most scholars disagreed.

Within a few years, the letter was largely forgotten. But when Mikhail Gorbachev suddenly opened up Soviet society to a measure of free discussion in the 1980s, the letter resurfaced as Russian historians resumed the discussion of Stalin's early career and his possible role as a police spy.

Historian and diplomat George F. Kennan wrote that the letter is "one of those curious bits of historical evidence of which it can only be said that the marks of spuriousness are too strong for us to call it genuine, and the marks of genuineness are too strong for us to call it entirely spurious."[13]

Among the aspects of the letter that raise the possibility that it is genuine is the extraordinary story of Stalin's 1906 arrest in Tiflis. Most accounts of Stalin's life make no mention of such an arrest. But one place it is mentioned is in Trotsky's unfinished biography of Stalin, which was published at about the same time as Levine and the White Russians began their quest to get the Eremin letter published. Trotsky's book—which rejected Stalin's possible role as an informer—nevertheless includes a chronology and notes his 1906 arrest.

If Stalin was arrested in 1906, it was probably during a police raid on the underground printing press in a Tiflis neighborhood called Avlabar. Like nearly everything else in Georgia then, this would have been a Social Democratic-controlled press. Stalin was one of the few Lenin loyalists in that region of the Russian empire.

But this was a time when Bolsheviks and Mensheviks across the Russian empire were temporarily forced to work together. Shortly after Stalin learned of the location of the Avlabar press, the police closed it down, making many arrests. Stalin may have been the one who tipped the police off.

Long before 1921, when he returned to Tiflis following the invasion of the Red Army, he was estranged not only from the Georgian Social Democrats but also from Georgia itself.

CHAPTER 6

The End of Independence

THE RUSSIAN BOLSHEVIKS WERE FOND of pointing out that the Georgian Social Democrats did not start out as nationalists. As Karl Radek, a leading figure in the Communist International, would later put it, the Georgian Social Democratic leadership "consists of men, not one of whom stood for Georgian independence before October 1917, but who were all Great-Russian patriots."[1]

Radek was not entirely wrong. Until the overthrow of the tsarist regime in March 1917, and more specifically, the Bolshevik seizure of power eight months later, the Social Democrats were among the least nationalistic of the Georgian political parties. Several parties were far more nationalist than the Social Democrats—including the Socialist Federalist Party and the National Democrats.

Like many other revolutionaries, the Georgian Social Democrats were certain that after the revolution, a new, democratic Russian republic would emerge and countries on the imperial periphery would get some kind of autonomy. There might be some exceptions, such as Poland and Finland, which would become fully independent. But most of the borderlands, including Georgia, would remain part of a future Russian federation.

The Georgian Social Democrats were not alone in holding this view. The Jewish Labor Bund also supported some autonomy for the Jewish people within a federated Russian republic. They described this as "nationhood without statehood," and they opposed the Zionists, who were advocates of an independent Jewish homeland, eventually to be created in Palestine. (Some of their rivals in the Russian Social Democratic Party called the Bundists "Zionists afraid of sea-sickness."[2]) The Bund has been described as "the largest socialist group in the Russian Empire" by 1906, though arguably the Georgian Social Democrats could claim that title too.[3]

While the Jewish Labor Bund and the Georgian Social Democrats were both successful mass movements and were both nationalist in some sense, neither supported national independence for their peoples.

So little did the Georgian Social Democrats care for nationalism that their first instinct when the Bolsheviks seized power was not to proclaim independence immediately. Initially, with their South Caucasian neighbors, Armenia, and Azerbaijan, they worked together as the "Transcaucasian Commissariat."

The political leaders in all three countries had hoped for a peaceful transition from the tsarist autocracy to a democratic, federal republic for the whole former Russian empire. But after the Bolsheviks came to power in Petrograd, particularly after they violently dispersed the Constituent Assembly in January 1918, it was clear that a Russian democratic, federal republic was not in the cards.

By April 22, 1918, with the Bolsheviks tightening their grip on power and no prospect of rejoining Russia, the three South Caucasian countries declared independence. They proclaimed a new state with the unwieldy name of the "Democratic Federative Republic of Transcaucasia." But it did not last, and within a few weeks, the three constituent republics went their separate ways. (The federation would be revived in a somewhat different form following the Soviet takeover of the region, as we shall see.)

Following the declaration of Georgian independence on May 26, 1918, and over the course of nearly three years of defending the country's newly won sovereignty from Turkish, Armenian, and Russian invaders, the Social Democrats (and indeed all Georgians) had undoubtedly become more nationalistic. Considering those developments, Soviet policy towards Georgia after February 1921 was, from the outset, problematic. Having had a taste of independence, the Georgians were not keen to return to being anyone's province. Georgian Bolsheviks were aware of this. And yet, the Soviets moved quickly to take on that new-found nationalism by putting a swift end to the country's independence. It was to be one of the factors that triggered ongoing unrest in the country and, ultimately, the nationwide uprising in August 1924.

The assault on Georgian independence began before the battles between the invading Soviets and the Georgian forces ended. As early as March 1921, Stalin's representative Sergo Orjonikidze met in Batumi with leaders of the Abkhaz Bolsheviks. Abkhazia was a Georgian province on the Black Sea coast. It was agreed that Abkhazia would be an "independent Soviet republic." Then, as now, Georgians viewed Abkhazia as an integral part of their country. But Orjonikidze valued the loyalty of the Abkhaz Bolsheviks and detested Georgian nationalism. In 1924, Abkhazians loyal to the Soviet regime played a role in suppressing the uprising in Georgia.

As for the area around Batumi, the province known as Adjara was given the special status of an autonomous Soviet republic in July 1921. This was done at the insistence of the Turks, who had a claim on the region.

The carving up of Georgia did not stop in Abkhazia and Adjara. The Soviets granted autonomy to South Ossetia, where Georgians and Ossetians lived side by side. The town chosen as the regional capital, Tskhinvali, had a Jewish majority.[4]

If the names of some of these regions (Abkhazia, South Ossetia) sound familiar, it is because the Russian army has occupied both areas in recent years. Both regions have declared their independence, though Russia is one of only a handful of countries to recognize them. Approximately 20 percent of Georgian territory is currently occupied by Russian forces.

The Soviets continued cutting up Georgian territory in 1921, giving some 12,000 square kilometers to the Turks, a big chunk of the Zakataly district to Azerbaijan, and another 4,000 square kilometers to the Armenians in the Borchalo district. The last of these was particularly painful, as back in 1918, the Armenians had invaded Georgia and were defeated in a short, bloody war. By early 1921, both Armenia and Azerbaijan were under Soviet control, and Moscow was rewarding those countries by carving up Georgia and dishing out parts of its land.

The Georgians were not silent about this. For example, the writer and poet Konstantine Gamsakhurdia published an open letter to Lenin. Let us keep our independence, he declared, or Georgia would become Soviet Russia's Ireland. (As we shall see, comparisons between Georgia and Ireland will also be made regarding the 1924 uprising.)[5]

But the Soviets were not listening. Instead of recognizing Georgia's independence (as the May 1920 treaty between Soviet Russia and Georgia obligated them to do), the Bolsheviks put an end to any hopes that Georgia might have some kind of independent status within a Soviet empire. The Georgian Bolsheviks, now led by Budu Mdivani who had been brought in by Stalin, were divided over the issue. Many understood that once they tasted independence, the Georgians would be unhappy with anything else. Donald Rayfield summed up what happened:

> A Soviet Central Committee commission listened to arguments between Sergo Orjonikidze, Stalin and Felix Dzierzynski, who insisted on federation, and

Budu Mdivani who represented the majority "nationalist deviationist" Georgian communists who opposed it.... Lenin, who regarded Stalin and Orjonikidze as typically coarse "Russified aborigines," sided with Mdivani, but was too ill to impose his will.[6]

Instead of welcoming a nominally independent Georgia into the Soviet Union, which was the case with Ukraine and other formerly independent states, Georgia was brought under the authority of a new Transcaucasian Republic, together with Armenia and Azerbaijan. Unlike the first, failed attempt in 1918, local politicians did not create this one. It was imposed by Moscow. The loss of independence was now made real and was one of the reasons for growing unrest in the country, as Gamsakhurdia predicted. It is also one of the factors that led up to the August 1924 nationwide revolt.

The dispute over independence inside the Georgian Communist Party grew to play an important part in Soviet politics in the final years of Lenin's life. As Moshe Lewin wrote:

The Georgian Communists were anxious to gain popular support in a Caucasus in which national and nationalistic feelings were particularly deep rooted and had recently been reawakened by the experience of independence under a Menshevik government that had just been crushed by force.[7]

The behavior of Orjonikidze, who was backed by the increasingly powerful Stalin, was described as being "proconsular." He dismissed the views of the Georgian Bolsheviks, including Mdivani. Lenin began to doubt the project of an imposed Transcaucasian Federation, preferring to try persuading the local population through a propaganda campaign. The Georgians had other allies in the Soviet leadership, most notably Makharadze, who although he was a lifelong internationalist, had his doubts about the plan to subsume Georgia under a regional government.

The Georgian Bolsheviks didn't just argue against Stalin and Orjonikidze's plan. They actively sabotaged it. Lewin wrote: "They installed military guards on the frontiers of the Georgian Republic, demanded residence permits, etc." They also passed resolutions in various government bodies, declaring "the inviolability of their national independence—resolutions whose antifederalist character was quite blatant."[8]

Orjonikidze's men accused their "nationalist" rivals inside the Communist party of a long list of sins. These included "closure of the border to non-ethnic Georgian refugees from the famine in Soviet Russia, their proposal for ethnic criteria for citizenship in the republic, their reluctance to hand over nationalized British oil reservoirs in Batumi to Azerbaijan, and their resistance to adopting Russian currency."[9]

A year after Georgia's conquest by the Red Army, Orjonikidze—with the support of the Communist leaders in Armenia and Azerbaijan—announced plans for a federal constitution that would mark the effective end of Georgian independence. With the support of Stalin, he waged war on the Georgian "national deviationists" throughout the year.

The Georgian Bolsheviks zealously defended what autonomy they had left. In a resolution passed by their Party's Central Committee, they decided "to consider premature the unification of the independent Republics on the basis of autonomization, proposed by Comrade Stalin's theses. We regard the unification of economic endeavour and of general policy indispensable but with the retention of all the attributes of independence."[10]

They were concerned, among other things, that while the proposed Transcaucasian federation might retain the right (on paper at least) to secede from the USSR, that right would be denied to the three constituent republics.

This led to a clash with the Transcaucasian regional Communist organization headed by Orjonikidze, which adopted a resolution supporting the federation plan. According to Lewin, they "used its superiority in the Party hierarchy to order the Georgian Central Committee to conform to Stalin's orders and not to make its divergences with Moscow public."[11]

On August 29, 1922, Stalin sent a telegram to the Georgian Bolshevik leader Mdivani informing him that the decisions of the highest governing bodies of the Russian Federation were binding on all the republics, including Georgia. The Georgians, realizing their weakness in the face of Stalin and Orjonikidze, appealed to Lenin for support—to no avail. But that was soon to change.

Running out of options, the Georgian Bolshevik leaders took an extraordinary step on October 22, 1922: they resigned collectively. As Lewin pointed out, "This was no doubt just what Ordzhonikidze had been hoping for," and he "immediately appointed a new Central Committee consisting of incompetent but docile young men who accepted the Federation without batting an eyelid."[12]

Orjonikidze's action backfired. According to Lewin, "The members of the old Central Committee did not give up the struggle. The change in leadership merely served to emphasise the unpopularity of Ordzhonikidze in his own country."[13]

Orjonikidze was losing his patience. In November, he physically struck another Communist Party member, who was a supporter of Mdivani. In another few years, such an event would not have been noticed as Stalin and his allies began killing Communists in their thousands. But in 1922, that kind of behavior inside the Bolshevik Party was considered inappropriate—and Lenin finally noticed.

Lewin wrote that "Ordzhonikidze was behaving like a Governor General, flouting legal and statutory considerations, using brute force against Communists of the national republics."[14]

As David Lang wrote:

> Following a spate of rumours and complaints coming in from Tbilisi ... an investigation commission headed by Felix Dzerzhinsky, head of the Soviet secret police, was sent to Georgia to report on the position there. Even the hardened Dzerzhinsky was horrified at the excesses committed by Orjonikidze and his associates under Stalin's orders.[15]

In Lenin's view, Stalin and Orjonikidze had crossed a line. Lang wrote:

> Dzerzhinsky's report contributed to Lenin's growing distrust of Stalin and his decision to exclude him from the future leadership of the Party. He resolved also to suspend Orjonikidze from party membership. In his Testament and other documents dictated shortly before his death, Lenin wrote that he "felt strongly guilty before the workers of Russia for not having intervened vigorously and drastically enough in this notorious affair." He was disgusted at the "swamp" in which the Party had landed over the Georgian business.[16]

On March 6, 1923, Lenin sent a message to the Georgian Bolshevik leaders. He promised to take up their case at the upcoming Party Congress. "I am with you in this matter with all my heart," he told them. He also wrote to Trotsky asking him "to undertake the defence of the Georgian affair at the Central Committee of the Party."[17] But four days later, a new stroke paralyzed half of Lenin's body and deprived him of the capacity to speak. Lenin's political activity was finished. He died on January 21, 1924, nearly a year later.

Stalin and Orjonikidze had won. Trotsky later described this as "the first victory of the reactionaries in the party."[18] The fate of Georgia as an independent country had been sealed.

CHAPTER 7

The Destruction of the Georgian Trade Unions

THE SOVIET VICTORY IN GEORGIA in 1921 led to the transformation of the country from a liberal democratic republic to a totalitarian state.

Though Mussolini would be among the first to use the term "totalitarian" in a positive way, Soviet Russia was the first genuinely modern totalitarian state. What it meant in practice, in the daily life of the Georgian people, was not simply regime change at the top with the old leaders sent into exile. It also meant a root-and-branch overhaul of civil society, leaving no space outside the control of the ruling Communist Party.

Totalitarianism sank roots in Georgia from 1921 onwards, including the destruction of the country's powerful and independent trade union movement. Developments like these contributed to rising anger among ordinary people and to the growing threat of a popular uprising against the Soviets. Under the tsarist regime, trade unions in Georgia were weak and only semi-legal. When that regime collapsed in 1917, the trade union movement rapidly grew. Strikes broke out in many different places. So frequent were those strikes that German soldiers, who occupied Georgia for a time, complained about them—especially strikes in the Black Sea ports.

As Donald Rayfield wrote:

> On 27 June [1918] the first consignment of manganese left Poti for Germany, but the shortage of dockers, and the undernourished, strike-prone state of those that did work, left more manganese behind than could ever be shipped. Similar blockages prevented the export of Abkhaz tobacco, highland wool and Kakhetian copper, or the import of much-needed flour.[1]

The Social Democratic government that ruled independent Georgia from May 1918 was very sympathetic to the unions and encouraged their growth. In developing their own early version of a "social mixed economy" to regulate prices and ensure that basic goods remained affordable, the Social Democrats made certain that unions played a central role in the process.

As the Constituent Assembly set about drafting a Constitution for the new Georgian Democratic Republic, the unions put forward one essential demand: the right to strike. It was accepted and Georgia became one of the very few countries in the world to recognize workers' rights as human rights. Even though Georgian workers, through their independent unions, had won a legal right to strike, they were so powerful that they hardly ever had to use it.

Following the Soviet invasion of Georgia in February 1921, the new Communist government imposed a totalitarian regime just as they had done in Russia. One of the first to feel the effects of this was the Georgian trade union movement.

In the previous three years, the Bolsheviks in Russia had debated among themselves what to do about the trade unions. As in Georgia, unions in Russia too had flourished in the aftermath of the fall of the tsarist regime. But it was clear to Lenin and his fellow Bolsheviks that trade unions must be under the control of the "proletarian vanguard"—in other words, the Communist Party. There was some debate about what this meant and how strict that control might be, but the Bolsheviks, for the most part, did not want workers to have independent unions controlled democratically by them.

Trotsky, based on his experience leading the Red Army to victory in the Civil War, proposed the militarization of labor as a solution to the problem of a low-productivity, broken economy. But his idea of an "army of labor" proved so unpopular that even Stalin thought it a step too far. In the end, the Bolsheviks settled for trade union organizations that were entirely controlled by the ruling party. Strikes did not take place. The main role of those unions was to act as a "conveyor belt" to pass orders on from the Party leadership to the workers.

Later on, they would also provide workers with things like inexpensive hotels for their holidays—ideas which were copied in Nazi Germany by the *Deutsche Arbeitsfront*, run by the notorious Robert Ley. Unions in the West referred to organizations like these, of both the fascist and Communist types, as "state-controlled labor fronts" and not as genuine trade unions.

Imposing this new system on the Georgian working class would prove to be a difficult task for the Communist regime. Stephen Jones described the difficult state of the Georgian economy which the Soviets inherited:

"Given such conditions and the long tradition of Menshevik support among the Georgian working class, it is hardly surprising that the new government faced considerable difficulty in securing a firm base among the workers. Menshevism, which in the Georgian context had become synonymous with national independence, remained a major force among Georgian workers until the mid–1920s."[2]

The genuine, independent, and democratic trade unions of Georgia did not go quietly into the night. "As organs for the defence of the interests of the working classes, they exist no longer," declared the Social Democrats in a message to a visiting German workers' delegation. "The Trade Unions in our country are only Government, bureaucratic institutions—neither more nor less."[3]

Without strong trade unions to defend them, the situation of the Georgian working class deteriorated quickly. "Exploitation of the Georgian working class under Soviet State capitalism does not in any way differ from the purely capitalist exploitation," wrote the Social Democrats. "The only difference that exists, however, is that the working class is now deprived of the right of demanding better working and economic conditions and of endeavouring to obtain them by means of strikes."[4]

The newly Bolshevized unions "not only do not try to improve the lot of the working classes, but on the contrary, they oppose together with the Government the economic demands of the workers; they are bureaucratic organs pure and simple of the Government; for the working class they are nothing but a financial burden, as the workers and civil servants have to contribute for the maintenance of the bureaucracy of the Unions 3 per cent and even more from their meagre earnings."[5] This really is the essence of the matter: without the right to independent trade unions and to strike, the position of the working class under "Soviet state capitalism" was weaker than it was under capitalism.

"The economic conditions of workers and other employees are daily getting worse. The wages or salaries they earn at present are not enough to buy even bare necessities," we are told.[6]

Despite the repression, the independent unions kept up an existence in the shadows, reaching out to foreign delegations that visited Georgia but rarely getting a hearing from them. This led to a sense of betrayal by those, including foreign trade union leaders, who should have been their allies. We shall see a particularly egregious example of this in the visit of the British trade union leaders in 1924.

While it was probably inevitable that the intelligentsia and the former nobility would oppose the Bolsheviks, the Georgian working class—which theoretically should have been a stronghold for the Communists—was also hostile to Soviet rule.

Combined with all the other problems faced by the new Communist regime, the alienation of the country's working class from its government meant that Georgia was now a ticking time bomb.

CHAPTER 8

The War on the Church

ONE OF THE ACHIEVEMENTS OF the Georgian Democratic Republic was overseeing the restoration of autonomy for the country's Orthodox church.

During its three years in power, the Social Democratic–led government generally took a hands-off approach to religious affairs. To the Georgian Social Democrats religion was a private matter. The Georgian Social Democrats did not attack the church in which so many Georgians had placed their faith, though they nationalized some church property, provoking some opposition.

In their attitude toward religion, the Georgian Social Democrats were following the example set by Social Democratic parties around the world. As the American Socialist writer John Spargo noted in his book *Marxian Socialism and Religion* (1915), "most of the Socialist parties of the world have at one time or another formally disavowed any hostility to religion and have pledged themselves to maintain complete religious freedom."[1]

As early as 1875, when some of Marx's followers together with other Socialists produced the Gotha Program of the German Social Democratic Party, they declared that "religion is a private matter." Spargo pointed out that in his own Socialist Party of America "at its national convention in 1908, incorporated in the party platform a declaration that religion must be treated as 'a private matter—a question of the individual conscience.'"[2]

Spargo even cited Karl Kautsky in defense of his view, writing: "Karl Kautsky, while stating as his personal view that the belief in a personal God and a personal immortality is irreconcilable with modern science, admits, nevertheless, that it is possible to be a good Christian and a Socialist at the same time."[3]

There were exceptions to the rule, including the fiercely secular French Socialist Party under the leadership of Jean Jaurès, but on the whole, the international movement to which the Georgian Social Democratic Party owed its allegiance and from which it drew inspiration never saw organized religion as its enemy. In independent Georgia during the years 1918–21, religion was indeed a private matter.

After the Soviet invasion of Georgia in February 1921, all that changed. The Bolsheviks did not agree with the traditional views of the Socialist Parties around the world, and they considered organized religion to be their enemy. Their goal, in Georgia as in Russia, was to confront and eliminate religious belief.

Sigmund Freud, who was no friend of organized religion, challenged the Bolshevik view a few years later: "It is certainly a nonsensical plan to seek to abolish religion by force and at a stroke. Principally because there is no chance of it succeeding. The believer will not allow his faith to be taken from him—not by arguments and not by bans."[4]

The Bolsheviks were not listening to Freud any more than they listened to Kautsky. Religion for them was not a "private matter." And they fully intended to abolish it "by force and at a stroke," to use Freud's words. As David Lang explained, "The Georgian Church was the object of special attention on the part of Stalin and his henchmen, who egged on mobs of hooligans to attack priests and loot the sanctuaries, in the course of which many historic relics and works of art were stolen or destroyed."[5]

The new Soviet government of Georgia waged open warfare against the Orthodox church, putting it once again under the authority of Moscow—and doing its best to reduce the church's influence in Georgia, especially among the young.

In early 1922, the anti-religious activities of the Communists prompted the new head of the Georgian Orthodox Church, the Catholicos Ambrose, to issue an open letter to the Allied Conference then meeting in Genoa, Italy. That conference ran over several weeks in the spring of 1922, and thirty-four countries sent delegations, though very little seems to have been accomplished there. But it was the largest conference of its kind since the Paris Peace Conference that followed the First World War and was seen as an important platform, not least for Georgians who had a message for the Western world.[6]

"Property, which has been soaked in blood and sanctified with the bones of its ancestors, is taken from the people and distributed among the invading aggressors," wrote Ambrose. "People's means of survival obtained through blood and sweat is taken away from them and sent abroad. They attack the mother language of the people, damage its national culture created by its ancestors, and even the most precious possession of the people, its faith, is being assaulted," he continued, combining criticism of the Bolsheviks' anti-religious activities with their broader anti-national agenda.

"Under a false banner of freedom of conscience people are forbidden to exercise their religious needs," he wrote. "Members of the clergy are being ruthlessly persecuted, our Church ... is now deprived of all its rights to the point that despite all its efforts the Church cannot obtain the means to provide for its survival."

As the Reverend Harold Buxton wrote in his 1926 book *Transcaucasia*, echoing Ambrose's letter: "Throughout the country the religious teaching of the young is forbidden. Large numbers of the clergy have 'disappeared'; and in many villages the ancient Churches have not merely been closed, or applied to secular uses, but have been deliberately destroyed. It is reported that in some districts the peasants have found means to erect new wooden buildings for worship. But for the most part, the young generation is growing up Godless—their minds poisoned against all religious thought and practice."[7]

Ambrose's letter to Genoa sent a powerful message, and it took tremendous courage for the Catholicos to send it. It infuriated the new Soviet regime in Tiflis. They were quick to act. As David Lang wrote, Ambrose "was immediately thrown into prison by the Communists and kept there until they imagined that his spirit was broken."[8] Ambrose and his "senior bishops were tried for treason in March 1924," wrote Donald Rayfield, "but revulsion at the executions of five senior clerics in Kutaisi in September 1924 forced [the] OGPU to reprieve Ambrosi and his bishops: they were sentenced to prison."[9]

The public trial of the church leaders did not go according to the Bolsheviks' plans. "The trial took place in a theatre in Tiflis, to attract the maximum publicity," wrote Walter Kolarz. "At its crucial stage a mass demonstration by four thousand workers was held in front of the theatre. The workers carried banners inscribed 'Down with the Catholicos' and demanding that the prisoners be condemned to death."[10]

This was exactly the strategy employed by the Stalinist regime during the show trials in the 1930s when groups of "ordinary workers" would demand the death sentence for formerly prominent Communist leaders who had been accused of treason. Ambrose and his colleagues were accused not only of sending out the "treasonous" letter to Genoa but also of concealing historic treasures of the Georgian Church to prevent them from passing into the hands of the Soviet state.

"The court proceedings were interrupted to hear the workers' delegates and to allow the presiding judge to address the manifestants, assuring them that exemplary punishment would be inflicted on the delinquents," wrote Kolarz.[11]

The show trial was not a success. According to David Lang, "the aged and venerated head of the Georgian Church demonstrated such moral fortitude that his ordeal turned into a great victory for his Church and nation. His concluding words were: 'My soul belongs to God, my heart to my country; you, my executioners, do what you will with my body.'"[12]

"At the end of this ten-day travesty of justice, the Catholicos and his co-defendants were found guilty of treason and deserving of death," reported Kolarz. "However, in view of the strengthening of the Soviet regime, said the verdict, it was possible to mete out milder punishment to the accused. The Catholicos was sentenced to eight years imprisonment, four priests received prison terms of from two to five years, and the rest were acquitted."[13]

They may not have killed the Catholicos, but the Cheka took revenge on his church. Over 1,000 churches were closed down, hundreds of priests and monks were arrested, and many of them were shot.

The Soviet government's war on the church in Georgia contributed to widespread discontent with the regime—discontent that culminated in the national uprising of August 1924.

CHAPTER 9

"The language of the bullet"

INITIALLY, THE BOLSHEVIK VICTORY IN GEORGIA was seen by some as an opportunity. Among these were several of Georgia's leading writers. On March 3, 1921, with the Social Democratic leaders heading into exile, the Bolsheviks made a clever move. They donated one of Tiflis' most beautiful mansions—it had belonged to the brandy merchant David Sarajishvili—to the Georgian Union of Writers and Artists. But the new rulers of Georgia "were extremely suspicious of the native intelligentsia which during the Menshevik period had come to accept the legitimacy of Georgian independence," according to Stephen Jones.[1]

The Communists aimed to impose a radical agenda in all spheres of state and public life, initially making use of "soft power" in an attempt to earn the respect of the country's artists and writers. This contrasted sharply with their approach to organized religion, which they suppressed ruthlessly.

But many Georgians were critical of their new Bolshevik rulers from the outset, including their perceived hostility to the Georgian language. In a resolution adopted in 1925 by the underground Social Democratic Party, reference is made to "the policy of the Communist Party, which is in itself anti-nationalist; it finds its expression, for instance, in the fact that the Georgian language has not up to the present been re-introduced in the State administration."[2]

One consequence of the Soviet policy towards the Georgian language, they reported, was that "the Georgian publishing business is dying a slow death, its market being swamped by Russian books; this is one of the consequences of the Russification policy."[3]

Sarajishvili's mansion in Tiflis remains to this day the Writers' House, and the building now contains a new museum dedicated to Georgia's "repressed writers." That museum begins with the story of Shalva Eliava, a representative of the Revolutionary Committee, which was the first Soviet government in Georgia. Eliava "explained the views of the new authorities to writers: if they cooperated with the regime, they would receive maximum assistance and comfort, but the government would not tolerate any dissent."[4]

Stalin's close ally Orjonikidze "made it even clearer to the Georgian intelligentsia that they should abandon their dreams of an independent Georgia, and that the Soviet authorities would respond to any attempts of sabotage with the language of the bullet."[5]

To writers who had grown used to the artistic freedom under the Social Democratic government, phrases like this—"the language of the bullet"—would have come as something of a shock. During the three years of the independent republic, many writers and artists who had fled Russia came to the thriving and free city of Tiflis. And even under tsarist rule, despite the censorship, a certain amount of artistic freedom had been tolerated.

As the Museum puts it: "Over the course of the 1920s, this framework—comfort in exchange for collaboration and repression in response to resistance—became the Soviet regime's main policy towards the artistic community."[6]

The fate of three Georgian writers during the first years of Soviet rule is indicative.

Just a few weeks after the fall of Tiflis to the Soviets, a memorial service was held for the fighters who died defending the city from the Red Army. After the service, the speakers were arrested by the Cheka. "Among them was the poet Ioseb Mchedishvili, who had read one of his own poems. This arrest is considered the start of the political persecution of writers by the new regime."[7]

The poet Davit Kopali was arrested on December 7, 1922, after he openly confronted Orjonikidze when the latter referred to Georgia's independence and history in what Kopali considered "insulting" terms. Kopali was released a few months later and withdrew from public life. Nevertheless, he eventually fell victim to the Great Terror of 1937.

Silibistro Remonidze, a writer, playwright, and publisher, was arrested by the Cheka in May 1923 for harboring underground Social Democrats. He was sentenced to two years in prison but was released after six months. But in 1936, he too perished in the first wave of the Stalinist terror.

Many more writers would be jailed and murdered during the long years of Soviet rule in Georgia. And it was not only writers and artists who found themselves in opposition to the new regime. As Stephen Jones wrote:

> The university of Tbilisi was seen as a hotbed of nationalism.... Of the 4,685 university students in 1928 only 65 were [Communist] party members. One Soviet historian claims that in the first years of Soviet power the overwhelming majority of "bourgeois students" took an 'active anti–Soviet position.' They led demonstrations in May 1922 to commemorate Georgian independence and many were active in the Menshevik youth organisation, the Young Marxists. The Georgian party paper *Comunisti* noted that most of those captured after the abortive 1924 uprising were between 15 and 25, although presumably not all were students. The university staff also resisted party influence; of the 103 faculty in 1924–25 none were communist party members.[8]

Jones summed up the fate of the Georgian intellectuals, writing, "Armed with wide powers of arrest, the Cheka and other organs of justice directed much of their early activity against the native intelligentsia and were often reprimanded for excesses."[9]

CHAPTER 10

The Peasantry
Under Soviet Rule

UNDER THE RULE OF THE ROMANOVS, the vast majority of the Russian Empire's inhabitants were peasants. Those peasants often lived in conditions of extreme poverty, the land was distributed unfairly, and peasant revolts took place from time to time. In the final years of tsarist rule, the Socialist Revolutionary Party grew into the largest party in the empire based on its support in the countryside, thanks to its commitment to giving land to the peasants.

Unlike the Socialist Revolutionaries, the Social Democratic Party—including both its Menshevik and Bolshevik factions—had little support among peasants. It was a party consisting mainly of urban workers and intellectuals. The party regularly discussed and debated its solutions to the problems faced by the peasants, but the peasants themselves were not part of those discussions. Except in Georgia.

The Georgian Social Democratic Party grew into a mass party with many thousands of members in large part because it successfully recruited peasants to its ranks. An early party rule banning peasants from membership was eventually tossed aside. Peasants were reclassified as "agricultural workers" and as *workers* they could become full party members.

In the run-up to the 1905 revolution, peasants in the western Georgian province of Guria rose up. For several years, they managed to run their territory without the interference of the Russian state. Guria was a Social Democratic stronghold, then and again nearly twenty years later when another rebellion challenged Bolshevik rule.

In 1917, following the abdication of the Tsar, power in Georgia fell into the hands of the largest political party, the one the peasants could be counted on to support—the Social Democrats. The Socialist Revolutionary Party, which in Russia dominated the countryside, won just 21,000 votes in the first Georgian elections, placing fourth.

The Georgian Social Democrats were acutely aware of the peasants' expectations. They also learned something from the Russian experience. In Russia in 1917, the promised agrarian reform was postponed until after the election of a Constituent Assembly. But those elections were delayed until after the Bolsheviks seized power. One of the many reasons for the lack of support shown for the provisional government in Petrograd was its failure to do anything to support the peasants, who had grown impatient.

In Georgia, following independence, the Social Democrats moved to swiftly implement an agrarian reform that would provide immediate benefits for the peasants. This helped keep the peasants on the side of the new government. The architect of the successful land reform in Georgia was the Social Democrat Noe Khomeriki, the Minister of Agriculture. Forced to flee with other members of the Georgian government at the time of the Soviet invasion, we will meet him again in 1924 when he secretly returned to the country.

The contrast between the successful agrarian reform in Georgia, with a government popular among the peasantry, and what was going on in Russia is striking. For the first three years of Bolshevik rule, the regime was at war with the countryside. The policy known as "war communism," which saw armed detachments sent out from the cities to seize food from the villages, resulted both in starvation in the cities and constant battles between peasants and the new Soviet authorities. It was not until early 1921 that Lenin came up with the "New Economic Policy" (NEP) which relaxed the rules, allowed some private trade to resume, and made the crisis less severe. Things were to get immeasurably worse when Stalin, in the late 1920s, launched his collectivization drive. That brought an end to the "New Economic Policy," causing the deaths of millions of innocent people across the Soviet Union.

The Soviet invasion of Georgia in early 1921 came at the end of the era of "war communism" and inevitably resulted in some of the same mistakes being made in Georgia as had been made across Russia in the first years of Bolshevik rule.

Stephen Jones described the new Soviet regime's approach to the Georgian peasantry:

> Immediately after the invasion emergency requisition measures were implemented to feed the cities and the death penalty was introduced for hoarding. (Bread almost disappeared from Tbilisi in June 1921.) A tax in kind (*prodnalog*) was introduced in July, which led to considerable peasant resistance;

it was reduced and modified in July 1922 to allow monetary payment. A land decree was published in April which contained all the features of the Russian model; nationalisation, confiscation above a certain norm without compensation and no buying or selling. The decree emphasised that poor and middle peasants would be untouched, and that money spent on buying their land under the conditions of the Menshevik reform would be returned. A system of *temebi* (local communes) and peasant land committees was set up to administer the reform. Although Georgian peasants were saved from the rigours of war communism, the conciliatory measures of NEP (New Economic Policy) which included the provision of credit and limited hiring and renting rights did not inspire any particular enthusiasm for the new regime. Despite the economic difficulties of the independence period, Georgian peasants had during this time already experienced economic freedoms similar to those granted by NEP.[1]

Saying that the new Soviet government "did not inspire any particular enthusiasm" for the Soviet state is surely an understatement. As the Georgian Social Democratic Party wrote in 1925: "The peasantry are groaning under the burden of taxation; in spite of repeated solemn promises the taxes have not been reduced. The arbitrary conduct of the Communist administrators continues unabated. The sale of agricultural produce does not cover in any appreciable way the requirements of the peasantry in manufactured goods."[2]

Donald Rayfield described the fate of the peasants under the new Soviet regime like this:

> Economic measures were more oppressive. In 1921 peasants were apportioned land according to family size and district.... Economic collapse, harvest failure in 1920, war in 1921 and the needs of an enormous occupying army of soldiers and Chekists caused widespread famine. Citizens' food stocks were requisitioned: Razhden Mirianashvili, a Tbilisi shop owner, was shot for withholding 44 pairs of socks; Novosiltsev, a Russian grocer, was shot for hoarding sugar and soap.[3]

Georgia, under Social Democratic rule, was not a Utopia; it was still a poor country facing many problems. But the arrival of the Soviets made things far worse, especially for the peasants.

By 1924, the Bolsheviks had managed to turn a large part of the countryside against the new regime.

CHAPTER 11

The Bolshevization of the Cooperatives

DURING THE THREE YEARS OF GEORGIAN INDEPENDENCE, the cooperative movement thrived. In some sectors of the economy, it even began to dominate. With the establishment of Soviet rule in 1921, the cooperatives, which had previously been independent of the state and run democratically, were brought under the control of the Communist Party.

While some leading cooperative activists fled the country after the Soviet invasion, those who stayed behind tried to defend the independence of their movement, resisting inside Georgia and inside the international cooperative movement too, where Bolshevik and Social Democratic leaders competed for recognition.

While arguably the peasantry, the trade unions, the intellectuals, the church, and the Social Democratic party constituted possible threats to the regime, why did the Bolsheviks feel the need to pick a fight with the non-political cooperative movement? This can only be understood as part of the process of asserting the total control of the Communist Party over civil society.

The first cooperatives in Georgia were established in 1867. The cooperatives were the first of the three great pillars of the labor movement to emerge in the country, with the trade unions and Social Democratic Party following much later. The Georgian cooperatives fell on hard times before and especially during the First World War but revived after 1917 and then grew dramatically. In 1919, the Georgian cooperatives reorganized themselves into *Tsekavshiri*, the Central Co-operative Union of the Republic of Georgia, dominated by consumer cooperatives.

Though consumer cooperatives continued to dominate, Karl Kautsky noticed a change when he visited the country in 1920. Producers' cooperatives were growing stronger. "The Union of Co-operative Societies began to produce on its own account in 1919," he wrote. "A silk factory is established, a sausage factory, engineering works, which turn out agricultural implements; then vegetable and fruit preserving factories, and finally a printing-press. None of these undertakings works at a loss, and most of them yield a surplus."[1]

The movement was growing and expanding beyond consumer and farmer cooperatives. All of this growth was taking place at a time of economic crisis in the country when private businesses struggled to make a profit. As a result, cooperatives were growing, and private businesses started disappearing. One survey discovered that private trading establishments in Georgian villages had declined from 2,071 to 1,479 as cooperatives moved "to take the places vacated by private capital."[2]

By 1920, only 19 percent of Georgian workers were employed by the private sector. A majority—52 percent—were employed by the state, and 18 percent worked for municipal or cooperative enterprises. The country was slowly transitioning from one based on production for profit to one resembling Robert Owen's vision of a cooperative commonwealth.

As the Georgian experiment was nearing its end, Karl Kautsky looked at what the Georgian cooperatives had done in just three years. He was delighted not only by how much they had achieved but also at the pace of their progress. "It is all to the good that the co-operative societies have proceeded slowly and cautiously in laying the foundations of their productive activities," he wrote.[3]

Following the Soviet takeover of Georgia in 1921, the cooperatives fell under the new government's control. The results were disastrous. "The real state of the cooperatives also appears to have been much worse than publicly admitted: 'they are really in a tragic condition and do not fulfill their purpose'"—according to one Soviet leader.[4]

Within a few months, leaders of the movement were being arrested. Rabinovich, a member of the Russian Trade Delegation in London and a former representative of Centrosoyus (the Soviet cooperative federation) in the Caucasus, wrote: "The first co-operative congress, in Georgia, after the advent of the Soviet Government, took place in November 1921. Up to that time, the old elected members of the Board of the Georgian Co-operative Union, with the exception of those who fled to Constantinople, remained in office." But this period of relative tolerance for the movement's former leaders was soon to end.

"The arrest of Mr. Andronnikov, chairman of the Board, and a Menshevik, had, to my knowledge, no relation whatsoever to his co-operative work,"

Rabinovich explained. Andronnikov's arrest "was due exclusively to the fact that he, along with other Mensheviks, was implicated in an attempt to organise a strike of railway workers, timed for the beginning of November."[5]

In other words, it was perfectly understandable to arrest someone for attempting "to organise a strike of railway workers"—as long as it was not because of his cooperative activities.

As the Bolsheviks tightened their grip on the Georgian cooperatives, the remaining non–Communist activists tried to use their leverage in the International Co-operative Alliance (ICA). A leading figure in that movement, the Belgian Victor Serwy, visited Georgia in the first half of 1922, just a year after the Red Army invaded the country.

The International Co-operative Bulletin in July 1922 mentioned that a delegation including Serwy and Gugushvili, a Georgian representative in London, had reached Tiflis "where they were pursuing their programme of establishing closer relations with our Georgian friends, and of seeing for themselves the conditions of the people stricken with famine for whom co-operators in various countries have contributed fairly considerable sums."

The Bolsheviks were furious at this visit. Rabinovich wrote in a pamphlet: "I may assure Mr. Serwy that during his journey in Georgia he was under the guidance not so much of Co-operators, as Mensheviks, who naturally did all they could in order that he might obtain the impressions which suited their purpose."[6]

By September 1922, the International Co-operative Bulletin reported how the fight within the Georgian cooperatives was spilling over into the international arena. In a report on a German cooperative congress, we learn that the Russian representatives from Centrosoyus "left the hall protesting because the President had allowed the Georgian delegate to speak."

In the view of the Soviet cooperative delegates, the Georgians were now members of Centrosoyus (thanks to the Red Army having conquered their country). They, therefore, had no right to an independent presence at a cooperative movement event, even in Germany.

According to one report, "The Congress loudly cheered the President's declaration that he had no right to prevent the delegate of any organisation that was a member of the ICA from speaking." At the time, the Georgian cooperatives were still members of the ICA.

Rabinovich, representing the Soviets, wrote a pamphlet responding to what Serwy had been saying about the state of the cooperative movement in Georgia.

"In the struggle which took place in Georgia between the two political parties, the Bolshevik and Menshevik, the victory fell to the former," he explained. "Many Georgian Co-operators are Mensheviks, and the defeat of their party naturally affected them too, but—this must be strongly emphasised—only as members of a defeated and irreconcilable party, and not in the least as Co-operators. When the defeated Menshevik Government of Georgia fled, a good many Co-operators who were their followers fled with them.... To this must be added the fact that among the Co-operators who remained in the country, there is still a considerable number of Mensheviks who, so far from accepting the defeat of their party, have continued, in pursuance of their political aims, to fight covertly the established Soviet Government of Georgia, and to keep in close touch with their political friends abroad."[7]

The reference to "a considerable number of Mensheviks" is unusually honest coming from one of Georgia's new Communist rulers, who at this time were insisting on the popularity of the Soviet regime in the country. By the time that a "considerable number of Mensheviks" took up arms in 1924, Soviet propaganda was asserting that these were small, isolated groups of bandits with no popular support.

In an argument echoing closely the words of Karl Radek, addressing the meeting of the three Internationals in Berlin in 1922, Rabinovich announced that "the Soviet Government in Georgia has in its possession documentary evidence which proves beyond any shadow of doubt that the Menshevik Co-operators in Georgia has [*sic*] received orders from their headquarters abroad to use to the utmost degree their influence in the Co-operative Movement in order to make it, as it were, the fulcrum in their fight for political predominance."[8]

The Social Democrats in the leadership of the Georgian cooperative movement were accused of being.... Social Democrats. As for accusations against the new Soviet rulers in Georgia, Rabinovich was dismissive.

"After the flight of the Menshevik Government, the position in Georgia, so far as Co-operation was concerned, was such that the Co-operative organisations could easily assume the leading role in the economic work of the country," he assured his foreign audience of cooperative movement leaders.

He didn't mention that under the Social Democrats, the cooperatives had already assumed "the leading role" he described. Georgia had been transitioning to a social mixed economy long before the Red Army invaded the country. "The accusations levelled against the Georgian Soviet

Government, that it nationalised the Co-operatives, have no foundation in fact," he declared. "The policy which, since early in 1922, was put into operation in Georgia in regard to Co-operation, was the new economic policy adopted in Russia," he said, referring to the liberalization of some parts of the Soviet economy introduced by Lenin after the colossal failure of "war communism."[9]

Rabinovich continued: "There can be not the slightest doubt that, had the Board of the Co-operative Union of Georgia showed a genuine desire to make use of its opportunities and embark upon active work, it could have secured a commanding position in the economic life of the country."[10]

The Georgian Soviet government was quite positive toward the cooperatives, he wrote. "As an indication of the actual attitude of the Georgian Soviet Government towards Co-operation, I may point out that at the time when all banks in Georgia were closed, the Government issued a decree, on June 1st, ordering the re-opening of the Co-operative Bank of Georgia, the Board of which was permitted to continue its work, in accordance with the old statutes of the Bank. The latter was actually re-opened and received back all its books. The Government, on its side, with a view to promoting and facilitating the work of the Bank, granted it credits."

Rabinovich was writing as an expert witness who had been in Georgia at the time. "During the summer of 1921, in my capacity as an accredited Representative of Centrosoyus in the Caucasus, I had two lengthy meetings with the Board of the above Co-operative Bank," he wrote. "I was interested to know why the Bank was showing no sign of activity and asked for an explanation."

The bank was inactive, he believed, because the Social Democrats still in Georgia, still active in the cooperative movement, were "hampering" the work of the new workers' and peasants' government. This happened despite the new government giving "every facility … to the Co-operatives to develop their work."[11]

A pattern was emerging in Soviet propaganda, especially concerning Georgia. There were "documents" that proved that all the bad things happening in the economy, including in the cooperative movement, were done deliberately by Social Democratic loyalists working under the orders of the government-in-exile in France.

In tightening their grip on the cooperatives, replacing Social Democrats and independents with loyal supporters of the new Soviet regime, one by one, all parts of civil society were coming under Communist control.

CHAPTER 12

Berlin 1922

MORE THAN FOUR YEARS AFTER the Bolshevik seizure of power in Petrograd, the gap between the Social Democratic and Labor parties and the newly formed Communist parties had widened. Those parties found they had less and less in common, each accusing the other of betraying the movement's values. But many on the Left still hoped for a reconciliation despite all that had happened.

On April 2, 1922, representatives of the three international Socialist organizations came together in the Reichstag in Berlin for several days of discussion and debate. The meeting in Room 25 was called by the so-called "Vienna" International (whose official name was the "International Working Union of Socialist Parties"). This group was also called the "Two and a Half International" because it sat politically between the Second International, founded in 1889, and the Third International, also known as the Comintern, founded by Lenin in 1919. The Vienna International was the strongest advocate for the reconciliation of the Social Democratic and Communist movements. And those movements were each keen to woo the Vienna International's parties, which were sitting on the fence.

The agenda for the conference would consist of just two points: the economic situation in Europe and working-class action; and the workers' defensive struggle against reaction. Georgia did not feature at all on the proposed agenda.

The leader of the Vienna International was Friedrich Adler, then 42 years old, from the Austrian Social Democrats. Adler commanded considerable moral authority among Socialists. As a protest against the First World War, in October 1916, he shot the Austrian minister-president Count Karl von Stürgkh in a hotel dining room in Vienna. Adler was sentenced to death, but he was freed from custody as the war ended.

On a cold and clear Sunday morning in Berlin, Adler had his work cut out for him. The Communists had founded their own International to compete with the Second International, which, in their view, had betrayed the working class by supporting the world war. The fissures began to appear as soon as the war broke out in the summer of 1914—it might be argued, even earlier. By the time the delegates assembled in Berlin, fully eight years had passed since they last sat together as comrades.

Adler opened the conference by noting its historic character—Socialists from the Second and Third Internationals had often found themselves on opposing sides of the barricades in the preceding years. Each side thought the other had blood on its hands. It would be difficult to have a conversation, let alone reunify the movements.

Friedrich Adler. His efforts to reconcile the Socialist and Communist movements collapsed when the subject of Georgia was raised (used by permission, AdsD der FES, 6/FOTA003647).

The delegates from the Vienna International included the prominent Austrian Socialist thinker Otto Bauer. Julius Martov, the leader of the Russian Mensheviks, attended, though he was already ill and would be dead within the year. Other official delegates came from Czechoslovakia, England, France, Germany, and Latvia. "Guests" sitting with the Vienna International's delegation included the Russian Menshevik Raphael Abramovitch and others from France and Germany. Two representatives of *Poalei Zion*, the Socialist Zionist party from Palestine, also sat with the delegation.

The Third International was represented by Clara Zetkin, the prominent German Socialist; Alfred Rosmer, the revolutionary syndicalist who had helped to found the French Communist Party; Sen Katayama, founding father of the Socialist movement and later the Communist Party of Japan; and others from Czechoslovakia, France, Poland, and Yugoslavia. There were two delegates from Russia: Nikolai Bukharin and Karl Radek. A leading figure in the Italian Socialist Party, Giacinto Menotti Serrati, sat with the Communists, though his party had not yet formally chosen sides.

Among the ten delegates from the Second International were four who had traveled to Georgia just a year and a half earlier: Emile Vandervelde and Camille Huysmans from Belgium and Tom Shaw and Ramsay MacDonald from Britain. They had been part of the international Socialist delegation to independent Georgia as guests of its Social Democratic government. Other delegation members included Ernest Bevin from the British Labour Party (the future Foreign Secretary) and others from Denmark, Germany, the Netherlands, and Sweden.

Irakli Tsereteli, a leading figure in the Georgian Social Democratic Party and a former minister in Kerensky's government, was also one of the delegates from the Second International.

This was a gathering of some of the best-known figures of the international Left—people like Bukharin, Bauer, Zetkin, and MacDonald were household names, at least in left-wing households. Several of those attending would later become government ministers in their countries and, in some cases, prime ministers.

A decade earlier, they were all members of the same broad church, the Second International. But by 1922, all that had changed, and it was remarkable that they were even sitting in the same room together.

Some leading figures on the left, notably Lenin and Trotsky from Soviet Russia and Karl Kautsky from Germany, did not attend the event. But even without them in the room, this was destined to be a historic confrontation.

The extraordinary thing about it was how quickly it descended into a fight over Georgia. This is certainly different from what anyone expected, or at least not what the Austrians who convened the event had expected. When Friedrich Adler opened the meeting, he spoke of it as an "experiment," concluding that "the mere fact that the Conference has met, which a short time ago would have seemed an impossibility, is already a measure of success."[1]

That was optimistic, as we shall see. The three Internationals were already deeply divided over various issues, some of which were addressed at the conference. Both the Second International and the Vienna International had their criticisms of how the Bolshevik government treated their comrades in Russia—including the banning of Socialist parties, the closing of Socialist newspapers, the jailing of their leaders, and so on. The presence of Tsereteli, Martov, and Abramovitch pointed an accusing finger at the representatives of a regime that had outlawed their party in Russia and, from 1921, in Georgia as well.

Adler spoke first, and Zetkin followed him. They over-ran the schedule. The delegates adjourned for lunch and resumed the discussion, with the next session chaired by the British Labour Party's Tom Shaw, who introduced the Belgian Social Democrat Emile Vandervelde as the first speaker from the Second International. Perhaps inevitably, Vandevelde's speech was explosive from the outset.

Expressing his skepticism about the possibility of convening a large international conference that all three Internationals would participate in—which is what was on the agenda—Vandervelde imagined how such an event might unfold.

"Socialist representatives from all the border States of Russia will stand up—from the Ukraine; from Armenia ... [and] from Georgia, where comrades forming a section of our International complain of what they call, I think rightly, Bolshevist imperialism? This will be the first discussion the day the Conference opens."[2]

Consider this for a moment: the leading spokesman for the Social Democrats, speaking on behalf of all the major parties of the European Left, including the British Labour Party, believed that the "first discussion" to be had with the Communist movement was about the fates of Georgia, Armenia and Ukraine.

Not the banning of the Socialist political parties in Soviet Russia, not the jailing of the Bolsheviks' left-wing opponents, not the establishment of the notorious Cheka and the labor camps, not even the brutal suppression a year earlier of the rebellious Kronstadt sailors—though most of these would be mentioned in time.

First of all, Vandervelde wanted to talk about Georgia and other victims of "Bolshevist imperialism."

He continued by posing several questions to the Communist leaders in the room. "If the Conference meets," he began, "will the peoples who are at present deprived of all right to determine their own fate, the Ukrainians, the Armenians, the Georgians, be put in a position which will enable them to elect freely their delegates to the general conference?"[3]

"I insist particularly upon the case of Georgia," he continued, no longer talking about Ukraine and Armenia. "And I speak of that primarily because I have seen it myself; I am an eye-witness, we are eye-witnesses; we ourselves have seen, during weeks which we can never forget, a people gathering unanimously—or almost unanimously—under the red flag, under the régime of free suffrage, electing an

Emile Vandervelde. Leading Belgian Socialist, member of the delegation to Georgia, who first raised the Georgian question at the Berlin meeting in 1922 (author's collection).

immense Socialist majority which wants to live, which has the right to live, and which we are determined to help to live."[4]

He spoke passionately on behalf of Huysmans, MacDonald, and Shaw, with whom he had traveled to Georgia in 1920. Those three knew precisely how he was feeling. The four had left Georgia only a few months before the Red Army invaded in February 1921. They had all written articles and given interviews where they talked about how wonderful Social Democratic Georgia had been. They had formed personal ties with Georgian Social Democratic leaders, including Tsereteli and Noe Zhordania.

Vandervelde had made his point. By raising the Georgian question as

Karl Radek. At the Berlin conference in 1922, he acknowledged that Soviet Russia had invaded Georgia—and helped to torpedo all talk of unity on the Left (author's collection).

he did, he ensured that two things would come out of this meeting in Berlin.

First, there would be no joint conference of the three Internationals and no unification of the Socialists and Communists. And second, the Vienna International, its efforts to reunify the Left having failed, would eventually fold itself back into Vandervelde's own Second International.

It fell to Karl Radek to answer Vandervelde in the name of Soviet Russia and the Communist International. Radek, now 36 years old, had spent his entire life on the far Left of the Socialist movement. Born in the city now known as Lviv in Ukraine, while still in his teens he was a participant in the 1905 revolution in Poland, where he was a member of the party headed by Rosa Luxemburg. He took Lenin's side in the internal faction fight inside the Russian party. He was a highly effective propagandist for the Bolshevik cause. Like Trotsky, he had written a book-length rebuttal to Kautsky's *Terrorism and Communism*.

Radek launched a blistering attack on Vandervelde and the Socialists. "With regard to Georgia," he said, "I do not know why Citizen Vandervelde"—he refused to address the Belgian Socialist leader as "comrade"—"should be so distressed because instead of" Social Democratic leaders including Zhordania, the Bolshevik Mdivani "has appeared in Tiflis or because Baku, that gate of invasion, is not in English hands."[5]

"I say to the representatives of the Second International, and especially to the English delegates: 'Hands off Georgia!' You did not protest when the Georgian government under the protection of English cannons massacred the peasants and workers of Georgia." At this point, according to the conference protocol, there were "contradictions and applause."[6]

The Soviet secret police, Radek said sarcastically, "are not talented men-of-letters." But the Georgians were different. They "were indiscreet enough, in the person of Mr. Dschugeli [*sic*] ... to leave behind them a book, and in this book, the Georgian democracy is presented in such a way that we will bring this book to the next Conference, so that you may learn that the Georgian State too was built of blood and iron."[7]

In other words, the Georgians did everything you accuse us of doing as well. And they bragged about it too—in books. The book Radek was referring to was the diary of Valiko Jugheli, the head of the Georgian National Guard. Trotsky also cited Jugheli's diary in his book-length attack on the Georgian Republic published after the 1921 invasion. The Bolsheviks liked to interpret Jugheli's diary as a kind of confession of "Menshevik crimes." Jugheli would go on to play an important—and tragic—role in the run-up to the 1924 rebellion, as we shall see.

Radek continued to compare the Georgian Social Democratic government to what followed under Communist rule. Still, in doing so, he blurted out something that previously had not been said, at least not in public: "And if you ask why—and now we say it openly—we helped to overthrow the Georgian Government, we will give you the answer from the documents which the Georgian Government was indiscreet enough to print."[8]

Until that moment, the Soviet Russian government had taken great pains to insist that the overthrow of the Georgian Social Democratic government was the work of the Georgian workers and peasants.

As the Georgian leader Noe Zhordania wrote in the first letter sent from exile to the Central Committee of his party, "We had to face the story disseminated by the Moscow government—there is no Russian army in Georgia, there was no war, the insurgents ousted the Menshevik government and elected the Bolsheviks."[9]

Of course, the Soviet leaders, Radek among them, knew perfectly well that they had invaded Georgia and that the story of a workers' revolution against the Social Democratic government in the country was fiction.

When Russia brazenly invaded Georgia in 1921, the regime's spokespeople, among them Trotsky, insisted that while the Red Army had provided some assistance, this was a genuine grassroots, popular revolution against a hated regime. And now, in Berlin a year later, Soviet spokesman Radek divulged the fact that "we" overthrew the elected Georgian government and added that "now we say it openly."

What was Radek up to? It appears that, like Vandervelde before him, the Soviet spokesman was doing all he could to ensure that there would be no further meetings of the three Internationals. That seemed to be the only thing the Social Democrats and the Communists could agree on.

And those Georgian documents Radek referred to? He cited one damning quote from a Georgian leader, saying: "We have helped the Whites; we have not only suppressed the Bolshevists in our country but have fed your White officers and sent them to you." Radek added: "If the Conference would like to set up a little commission to prove the authenticity of this document, we will very gladly submit it to them."[10]

Radek's proposal to set up a "little" commission to authenticate a document that "proved" the guilt of the Georgian government, which had always claimed to be neutral in the Russian Civil War, was taken seriously by no one. It was never mentioned again.

The conference resumed the following morning with Clara Zetkin in the chair. Zetkin, too, will play a role in the story of the aftermath of the August 1924 uprising in Georgia—we will meet her again.

The first speaker, on behalf of the Second International, was British Labour leader Ramsay MacDonald, who, like Vandervelde the previous day, had been part of the international Socialist delegation to Georgia in 1920. "In the case of Georgia," he said, "there is something essential: though its sins be as scarlet, I am not at all sure that if we appointed an impartial commission, it would be very easy to establish your claim that you are saints."[11] In his reference to scarlet sins, MacDonald was citing the Old Testament (Isaiah 1:18), but he omitted the words that preceded these: "Come now and let us reason together."

There was no coming together and no reasoning in Berlin that week.

"The essential fact is that Georgia had a Socialist Government," MacDonald continued. "The party in Georgia responsible for that Government is affiliated to us; the party in Georgia responsible for that Government is represented here by a delegate sitting at this table"—meaning Irakli Tsereteli.[12]

"You suppressed it by military force. You hold your position now there to-day by military force. We say: How can we act together until the Government for which we are responsible is re-established—or at any rate until the military occupation which has excluded them from the country is withdrawn and the people of the country have a chance of saying whether they want you or us."[13]

MacDonald made one last doomed attempt to "come now and reason together" with the Communists, saying: "I put it to you: is not our position the only position that men of common sense could take up when discussing the possibilities of future action? We offer you a proposal: send a commission representative of Socialist tendencies; give them a chance to enquiring and issuing a report. I can assure you, so far as we are concerned, if such a commission goes, it will go impartially for the purpose of discovering the truth. We ask for an honest enquiry."[14]

The Italian delegate, Giacinto Menotti Serrati, was in the strange position of representing a party affiliated with none of the three Internationals. Some thought his neutral party could host the proposed big conference of the three Internationals if agreed upon. When it was his turn to speak, he, too, raised the question of Georgia.

"Let us examine the second condition," he said. "It concerns the liberty of Georgia."[15] One imagines that he used the term "liberty" sarcastically because the remarks that followed were a blistering attack on the Social Democrats, especially Vandervelde. Serrati accused the Belgian of hypocrisy, caring nothing for the self-determination of nations before and during the world war.

"Now it is a case of Georgia, the case of a people whose Socialist Party belongs to the London [Second] International. And then you say: 'Liberty for peoples to determine their own fate.'"[16] Serrati thought that the Georgians had been turned into little more than tools in the hands of the imperialists.

"We have met the problems of Georgia, Armenia, Azerbaidjan [*sic*], Persia and all the other countries of the Near East before," he said. "I think that socialists have known them for a long time"—and they have learned that "small peoples may become, at a certain moment of international imperialist politics, mere tools in the hands of international capitalism to work for capitalist and not for proletarian interests."[17]

The idea that small countries could be "mere tools in the hands of international capitalism" was adopted by the Soviet regime and survives even today in the Russian approach to countries like Ukraine, which are still seen as "mere tools" in the hands of the West.

Serrati rejected the commission of inquiry that Ramsay MacDonald had proposed. "Do you think," he asked, "it will be possible to resolve a problem, which is a century-old problem by means of a commission of enquiry, meeting under artificial conditions and unable to judge fairly, as has happened with all commissions of enquiry?"[18]

Serrati followed this with what has to be one of the earliest and purest examples of what has become known as *what-aboutism*.[19] "And why a commission of enquiry for Georgia," he asked, "and not, for example, for Upper Silesia, Tunis, Algeria, Tripoli, the Congo, etc.?"[20]

Of course, Serrati was not proposing that the three Internationals investigate what was going on in the Congo—and one wonders if Serrati himself actually had a view on the subject or if he was randomly throwing out names of other "small peoples" who deserved attention just as much as the Georgians did. He asked the Social Democratic leaders if their interest in the South Caucasian country was "simply because you have a representative of the Georgian Socialists in your London International?"[21]

He wasn't entirely wrong. It *was* because the Georgian Social Democrats had long played a prominent role in international Socialist politics that leaders like Vandervelde and MacDonald became more aware of Georgia's plight. The prominence of Georgian Social Democrats was why the European Socialist leaders—including Karl Kautsky—visited the country just 18 months earlier.

Serrati's argument could equally have been made by any of the Communist delegates—which is not surprising as he had been a Communist, then returned to lead the Italian Socialists and would later return to the Communist fold. But at this point, he paused his attack on the Social Democrats and resumed his role as the "unaffiliated" Italian Socialist.

"It is true that there are grave problems in a country which was administered by a Socialist Government, or one which called itself Socialist, and which has been invaded by the army of another Socialist Government, or one which calls itself Socialist," he said.[22]

Instead of the relatively modest proposal by the Second International to establish a commission of inquiry—a proposal far more moderate than what they could have demanded, such as the immediate evacuation of Soviet Russian forces from Georgian territory and the restoration of Georgian sovereignty—Serrati had a better idea.

He proposed unity of all the Internationals. "If ... we remain together, begin to build up this unity of front, this unity will make it possible for us to resolve, not only the Georgian problem but all other problems that can be solved under a capitalist regime," he said.[23]

In other words, there were to be no preconditions before a general conference, no barriers to the unity of the Internationals, and no commission of inquiry regarding Georgia.

Later in the day, it was the turn of Austrian Socialist leader Otto Bauer to speak. His Vienna International had convened the conference, and he was desperately trying to hold things together as it was all falling apart.

"The task we have set before us at this Conference," he reminded the delegates, "is to bring together the three armies into which the proletariat has been unfortunately divided so that they may be able once more to march together against the common enemy, and, united, defeat that enemy."[24]

Things were not going well, as Bauer well knew. Though he and his Austrian comrades wanted the reunification of the Internationals more than anything else, raising the Georgian question touched on a sore spot. "All the organisations united here should respect the right of peoples to self-determination, and ... the right of self-determination in the case of the Georgian Republic has been violated."[25]

He then turned to the previous speaker's remarks, the Italian Serrati, who, according to Bauer, "has spoken somewhat sceptically about the right of peoples to self-determination." Bauer clarified, saying, "I cannot agree with him there."[26]

"We German-Austrians," Bauer said, "who have suffered ourselves because our bourgeoisie tried to dominate other nations and violate the right of self-determination, we support this principle absolutely, and go so far as to consider that even a partial success in the direction of the liberation of peoples is an historical step forward."[27]

His support for the self-determination of peoples was unconditional, and answering what Radek and Serrati had said, he emphasized that support "although it may be used at the moment by one imperialism or another for its own ends." Having asserted the principle that the Austrian Social Democrats had long advocated, based on their own experience living in a multi-ethnic empire, Bauer turned to the issue at hand. "On these grounds alone," he said, "it can be seen there is no divergence of opinion between us and the Second International on the question of Georgia."[28]

Not long after the Berlin conference ended, reconciliation between the "Vienna International" and the London-based "Second International" would accelerate, eventually leading to their reunification as the "Labour and Socialist International"—excluding the Communists. At this moment, in Bauer's remarks on Georgia, we can see this process already underway.

"We admit, however, that the case of Georgia stands apart from all these others [violations of self-determination] because here there are proletarian and socialist parties on both sides, who were responsible for what happened; because it was an army flying the red flag which in this case supported the military occupation; because whenever the proletariat now raises a protest against the violent deeds of imperialism, it is met with a scornful reference to Georgia."[29]

At this point, Bauer's remarks triggered shouts of "Quite right!" from both the Socialist delegations. "I have gone further, then, and said that the case of Georgia is in quite a different category from other cases of the violation of the right of peoples to self-determination," he continued.[30] But now, having come down hard on the Communists and true to the spirit of the Vienna International, Bauer turned his fire towards the Social Democrats.

"But however true this may be, comrades of the Second International, can you seriously say that in every case of the violation of the right of peoples to self-determination which we have experienced since 1918 Socialist Parties, to which you have belonged and, in some cases, still belong, have not also been responsible?"

"If this is a moral condition, which I admit, for the united front of the proletariat and all the proletarian parties, that self-determination of peoples shall be respected [and] this certainly applies to Georgia."

"But," he added, "it also applies to a whole number of other cases where the principle has been violated by Governments in which Socialist Parties participate, which are affiliated to you, comrades of the Second International."[31]

It was now Karl Radek's turn to reply. Again, Georgia, came up very quickly. He answered Ramsay MacDonald: "For him, only England exists. England always stands for small peoples unless she has conquered them. But on the other side, there is another State, and this other State has devoured poor innocent Georgia, and still, other States have been eaten up too."

The sneering reference to "poor innocent Georgia" would not have gone unnoticed.

Radek went on to ask MacDonald: "You were a member of the Second International before the war: 'Why did the Second International never demand the independence of Georgia before the war in the days of Tsarism?'"[32]

Radek was being completely disingenuous—he knew full well how Georgia was transformed from a province of the Russian Empire to an independent republic. In May 1918, the Georgian Social Democrats decided on independence only after Lenin and the Bolsheviks had seized power in Russia and dispersed the elected Constituent Assembly. It was not what they had intended, but it seemed the only possible choice. Radek also knew the position of Lenin and the Soviet state regarding the right of nations to self-determination, including secession, even if that commitment was honored more in the breach. Radek then proceeded to deliver a history lesson on Georgia.

"As you know," he began, "the present champions of this freedom are the Menshevik Government of Georgia, which we overthrew."[33] Again, he said it—no more pretense about a local rebellion that reached out to Soviet Russia for assistance. "We"—the Russian army—overthrew the Georgian Social Democrats and forcibly annexed their country.

That Social Democratic government, now in exile, Radek continued, "consists of men, not one of whom stood for Georgian independence before October 1917, but who were all Great-Russian patriots." He then turned to the one Georgian in the room, Tsereteli, speaking about his role in 1917 as a Minister in the Provisional Government headed by Kerensky. The Georgian, he said, "fought so vigorously for Great-Russia that he took part in the 1917 offensive" against the Germans, and not only that. According to Radek, Tsereteli "was the only member of the Russian Soviet to vote for the death penalty against the soldiers because he thought [it] necessary for the defence of Great-Russia."[34]

Radek argued that Tsereteli's support for the death penalty for soldiers during the war meant he had no right to speak out on the killings of unarmed civilians by Soviet Russia during peacetime.

This was all rather far removed from the question of the Soviet Russian occupation of Georgia. Radek then tried to drive a wedge between the two "Menshevik" groups at the conference, pointing out that the Russian Martov and the Georgian Tsereteli had different views about this issue. Martov had led the anti-war faction of the Russian Mensheviks, while Tsereteli served in the Provisional Government, which continued the war.

The wedge Radek was trying to drive between the Georgian and Russian Social Democrats had some basis. After the 1924 uprising in Georgia, there was a public rift between the two parties over how Socialists should react to armed uprisings against the Bolshevik regime.

To Tsereteli, and more broadly to the Georgian Social Democrats, Radek fired off this accusation: "To you who stood first for the independence of Georgia when it was a question of attacking the [Russian] Workers' Republic, what have you done with your independence?"[35] And then he answered his question: the Georgians used their independent republic to repress the local Bolsheviks (of whom there were very few) and to support the Whites during the Russian Civil War (which was not true—Georgia was neutral).

Radek continued: "You tried to root out the Bolshevists with blood and iron. I can read you a declaration by your Foreign Minister, Gegetchkori, to [Russian White] General Alexejev at a Conference with the representatives of the White armies of the South: 'We have suppressed the Bolshevists in our country, we have given shelter to your White officers.'"[36] He was repeating what he had read out the previous day, keen to make the point that Georgia was a tool in the hands of those fighting to overthrow the Soviet government in Russia.

"If you doubt this declaration," Radek continued, "we have the collection of documental [sic] reports of your government, which fell into our hands when we took Tiflis."[37]

"When we took Tiflis"—yet another acknowledgment that it was the Red Army that invaded and occupied Georgia, something which, until that day, the Soviet Russian government had taken pains to deny. Radek had much more to say—and remember that this was at a conference that aimed to reunite the three Internationals by fighting against reaction and building workers' resistance to right-wing governments.

Radek was having none of that. He wanted to keep talking about Georgia. "What about this independence then?" he began. "On the invitation of the Georgian Government came General von Kress, the famous German 'deliverer' of Georgia. I understand the tragedy of your position with regard to the bands of the Turks," he continued.[38] Radek was referring to the Georgian government's decision in May 1918 to invite in the Germans as protectors to prevent an imminent Turkish invasion.

"But that does not say that Georgia was independent," he continued. "When you invited the German troops, you said: 'We cannot stand alone in the world'—and you formed a coalition with the German Government. You went out to meet the German troops and, together with the German officers, shouted hurrahs in honour of the deliverers, in honour of German imperialism."[39]

This was a bit much, considering that earlier that same year (1918), Soviet Russian negotiators gave away vast swathes of their country to Germany under the Brest-Litovsk peace agreement. Those territories were handed over to the Germans, with the Soviets losing all authority there, unlike in Georgia, which retained its independence despite the presence of German troops in the country.

"Then the Germans disappeared," Radek continued, "and General Thomson appeared, and with him, the much cleverer, more subtle English occupation. They left their cannons and their army in Batoum."[40]

Radek then read a declaration by the Georgian President, Noe Zhordania, in which he said, "We cannot remain neutral, and if we have to choose between Eastern fanaticism and Western civilisation, we decide in favour of Western civilisation."[41]

In the end, Radek turned to the questions posed at the outset by Vandervelde and the Social Democrats. The first of these was the proposed commission of enquiry. "We agree to this condition, which [is] not a condition.... Before I read it," he said, "I had referred in my speech to the examination of documents by a commission."[42]

The Communists could not simply agree to the proposed international commission of inquiry. Radek made this clear when he said, "I would like to ask whether in 'similar circumstances' the attitude of the Labour Party towards the Egyptian question, the Irish question, and the Indian question ought not to be examined."[43] He had forgotten Upper Silesia, Tunis, Algeria, and the Congo.

The conference's final session ended on Wednesday, April 5, opening many hours later than planned—at a quarter to midnight. Friedrich Adler reported that the three Internationals had reached an agreement on a statement, which he read out. The short statement agreed upon by the three Internationals included this paragraph:

> The Conference declares that all the three Executives have expressed their readiness to collect and examine the material to be submitted by the different sections on the question of Georgia. The Conference authorises the Committee of Organisation to draw conclusions from this examination and to present a report to a later Conference of the three Executives.[44]

But even this very tame resolution resolved nothing; the three Internationals ceased all cooperation shortly after the Berlin meeting and never convened again.

The invasion and occupation of Georgia by Russia's Red Army ensured that there was to be no unity between the various Socialist and Communist Parties in 1922. The Berlin conference had failed. The final nail in the coffin of "unity" between the left parties would come two years later following yet another bloody Soviet Russian military operation in Georgia.

But before that could happen, the Soviets needed to deal with the stubborn persistence of the Georgian Social Democratic Party.

CHAPTER 13

The End of Georgian Social Democracy

MORE THAN TWO YEARS AFTER the Soviet invasion of Georgia, the new regime in Tiflis faced mounting problems. The Social Democratic Party refused to disappear despite efforts by the Cheka to destroy it. The party not only survived but grew. As Trotsky wrote, "In Georgia, premature sovietisation strengthened the Mensheviks for a certain period."[1]

That strengthening of the Social Democrats came at a cost to the Communists, who were increasingly unpopular for several reasons, which we have noted. These included suppressing the political opposition, crushing the independent trade unions, and waging war on the church. Stalin and Orjonikidze's heavy-handed decision to incorporate Georgia against its will in a new Transcaucasian federation, which triggered the resignation of the entire Georgian Communist Party's Central Committee, did not help make the new Communist regime in Tiflis more popular.

To secure Soviet rule in Georgia, it was necessary to once and for all bring an end to the party that had ruled the country for just three years, the Social Democrats. This was proving to be a more complicated problem than previously thought.

Eventually, the Georgian Bolsheviks found a solution—one that would not only work in Georgia but elsewhere as well. In the years to come, it became a template for Communist governments anywhere in the world that faced the problem of a stubborn and popular Democratic Socialist opposition.

The popularity of the Georgian Social Democrats among the peasants and other classes posed a real problem for the new Soviet regime in Georgia. Initially, the Social Democrats were persecuted, but their party was not entirely outlawed. For the first thirty months after the Red Army invasion, the Social Democrats and other opposition parties enjoyed a shadowy, semi-legal existence.

This was partly because Lenin himself had encouraged the local Bol-sheviks to tread lightly, aware of the popularity of the former ruling party, many of whose leaders had left the country in 1921, though most stayed behind. As one Soviet historian put it, "Lenin called on the communists of Georgia and the Caucasus as a whole, not to follow stereotyped tactics and to display 'more mildness, caution, and pliability with respect to the petite bourgeoisie, the intelligentsia, and particularly the peasantry."[2]

Lenin's awareness of the unique character of the Georgian Social Democracy led to his decision to oppose Stalin and Orjonikidze's heavy-handed rule over the country. Lenin and Trotsky sided with the local Georgian Communist leaders in their fight for greater autonomy precisely because they knew the Moscow-led Bolsheviks had not sunk deep roots in the country. The new rulers needed to proceed with some caution to plant those roots.

But the new regime in Tiflis could not for long tolerate the existence of independent political forces and, in particular, the Social Democrats, who competed for their support among workers and peasants. Among other concerns, the risk of an armed uprising was becoming more real. And no one understood this better than Stalin, who, following his disas-trous visit to Tiflis in 1921, "ordered the liquidation of all remains of the Georgian Menshevik party."[3]

The order did not produce the results he had hoped for. Social Demo-crats continued their work from abroad as the party kept open communi-cations channels with those left behind in Georgia. The Social Democratic party in exile protested against and publicized the ongoing repression, going so far as to describe the Bolsheviks as behaving like Fascists.

"The persecution of our Party continues with the same vigour," they wrote in a report to Social Democratic parties elsewhere in the world. "Flogging of political prisoners and torturing of our comrades in the dark and deep dungeons of the Cheka continue unabated. The Communist Party and Cheka employ Fascist methods against the members of our Party, shooting them from behind. (Example: The murders of comrades Alpaidze and Pkhakadze in Koutais.)"[4]

Two years after Orjonikidze boasted to Lenin that the red flag was fly-ing over Tiflis and that independent Georgia was finished, the Social Dem-ocrats and their allies were planning their return to power.

The Communists decided to try new tactics to bring an end to the Social Democrats. First, they encouraged people to resign from the party.

It had some limited success. As Ronald Suny wrote, "From Paris, the exiled Central Committee of the Georgian Social Democratic Party issued a statement denouncing the resignations of Mensheviks, which they claimed were the result of coercion and persecution by the Cheka."[5]

Some brave party members stood up against the campaign to force resignations. At a meeting in Tiflis, one Targamadze denounced the Communist effort to destroy the party, saying that the campaign was "carried out by threatening workers with loss of work, imprisonment, the 'basements of the Cheka' and exile."[6]

Targamadze said the Social Democrats had 50,000 members before the 1921 Soviet invasion of Georgia. They had, he claimed, hundreds of thousands of supporters. He continued: "After the Sovietization of Georgia, not only Mensheviks but the whole people were hostile to the Communists, and, I will say openly, they were ready to fight against them.... Instead of a dictatorship of the proletariat, a dictatorship of a bunch of people, a group of people over the proletariat."[7]

As Suny summarized the meeting, "Other speakers denied that they had been coerced to renounce Menshevism, but it seemed clear that two years of Bolshevism in Georgia and the probability that Russian backing would keep the new government in power made recantation a more realistic alternative to holding unfurled the Menshevik flag."[8]

The Communists would describe the Georgian Social Democratic leaders as "cowards" who fled the country rather than fight. One could still hear this said in Tbilisi decades after Georgia regained its independence in 1991. But at the time, in the early 1920s, the exiled Social Democratic leaders did retain their popularity in Georgia. According to Suny, "The reports from the conferences indicate that sympathy for the old social democratic leaders remained intact. Zhordania's name evoked applause."[9]

Meanwhile, the new Soviet regime organized a play to tour the Georgian provinces to encourage hostility toward the exiled Social Democrats. It was called "Mensheviks in Paris." It did not achieve its goal and was denounced for attacking the former President, Noe Zhordania. Even resolutions passed at conferences that accused the Social Democrats of being counterrevolutionaries had to be modified. Memories of the Georgian Democratic Republic and its leaders were still too fresh in peoples' minds.

While some Social Democrats caved under pressure and quit the party, others remained loyal. The Communists came up with a new and radical idea to solve the problem.

In August 1923, the Georgian Communist government compelled the Social Democrats to dissolve their party themselves. A conference had been held in Moscow two months earlier with representatives of the various national borderlands in attendance. As a result of that, a campaign was launched in Georgia to finally liquidate the remaining Social Democratic groups. Local conferences were held with the participation of former Social Democrats, including a prominent former Russian Menshevik, Aleksandr Samoilovich Martynov.

Technically, the party holding its congress in Tiflis in August 1923 no longer existed. It was outlawed and dissolved in 1921. And yet it still claimed some 11,000 members across Georgia. The Soviet authorities could no longer pretend that it didn't exist. It was allowed to convene but for one specific purpose: to dissolve itself.

Among the speakers sent to address delegates was one of the legendary figures of Georgian Marxism, Filipp Makharadze. Makharadze was then 55 years old. He was a contemporary of Noe Zhordania, and like the Social Democratic leader, he came from the rebellious rural province of Guria. Like Stalin and many other revolutionaries, he had studied at the Tiflis Theological Seminary. He knew the history of the Georgian Social Democracy from the inside. Unusually for a Georgian Social Democrat, he sided with Lenin and the Bolsheviks when the Russian Social Democratic Labor Party split.

The Bolshevik Makharadze was honest about the state of his party in Georgia. "In a secret report, which was later published in the press, he mentioned the unpopularity of the Bolsheviks," according to Georgian historians and archivists.[10]

Makharadze came before the Social Democrats with an interesting message. Instead of railing at them as agents of British and French imperialism or allies of the defeated White armies with their reactionary agendas, as was the Soviet style, Makharadze tried flattery. He praised the work of the Social Democrats in the early years, especially during the 1905 revolution. He said that enough bad things had been said about the Social Democrats (by his party, the Bolsheviks) and that it was now time to acknowledge their past services.

But he added—as he had to—that the Social Democratic Party had "taken a definitely false path during the world war and the February Revolution and found itself in the camp of counterrevolution."[11]

Martynov, too, addressed the delegates. At 58, he was even older than

Makharadze and had begun his political career in the populist "People's Will" party in the 1880s. He spent a decade in Siberian exile before joining the Social Democrats. Unlike Makharadze, Martynov chose the Mensheviks when the Russian party split, and he was closely allied with Julius Martov, the "Internationalist" faction leader who opposed the First World War. He switched sides and became a Bolshevik during the Civil War, becoming a full member of the Russian Communist Party in 1923.

Martynov tried to explain to the Social Democratic delegates why he had abandoned his previous comrades and joined the Bolsheviks—and why they should as well.

"In the October days history placed before us the question: for a dictatorship of the proletariat or for democracy?" he told them. Many years later, Communists would no longer speak so directly in these terms. They would refer to the 1936 Stalin constitution as being "the most democratic in the world" and would call the Soviet-sponsored dictatorships in Eastern Europe "people's democracies." But in 1923, they still spoke openly about how dictatorship was superior to democracy.

Trying to justify his break with the Mensheviks, he invoked Martov's name. "You see, comrades," he said, "my break with the Menshevik party is only the logical outcome of that struggle which Martov and I carried on within this party for many years against its opportunism." The implication was that Martov too would have eventually joined the Communists. Martov had died four months earlier and could not reply.

Martynov continued, saying that "the only thing that kept me from breaking with it [was] the prejudice that the road to the victory of socialism lies through democracy and not through dictatorship."

But that commitment to democracy was rapidly weakening, said the former Menshevik leader. "When I found myself in Ukraine, on the front line, in the very cauldron of counterrevolution where revolutionary and counterrevolutionary elements clashed, it became completely clear to me that the revolution can win only by means of iron-willed and ruthless dictatorship. Then the last obstacle separating me from the Communist Party fell away."[12]

Whether it was the persuasive arguments of the Georgian Bolshevik Makharadze, the former Russian Menshevik Martynov, or the Cheka's threats, the delegates voted to disband the Georgian Social Democratic Party. The Communist strategy had worked, and it would be tried again in other countries.

Twenty-two years later, at the end of the Second World War, the German Communists faced a similar problem. Elections in November 1945 in Austria produced disastrous results for the Communists. Realizing that the same thing might happen to the German Communist Party (the KPD), they contacted the Social Democrats (SPD) to suggest reuniting the two parties. The initial attempt at unity did not go well. The SPD held a vote in the western-controlled parts of Berlin in early 1946, and 82 percent voted against unity with the Communists. Realizing that something similar might occur in the Soviet-controlled part of Berlin, the German Stalinists learned from the Georgian experience of 1923.

"On 21 April 1946, a unity conference was held uniting SPD members in the Soviet zone and East Berlin into the newly formed German Socialist Unity party (SED)," wrote Julius Braunthal.[13]

He continued:

> With this decision the seal was set on the fate of Social Democracy in the five districts of the Soviet Zone. In these areas, the S.P.D. had been able to claim 619,000 members, many thousands of whom were no doubt against integrating their organization with the Communist party. But now there would never be any question of their being able to separate out again from the S.E.D. and to reconstitute themselves as the S.P.D., since the Soviet occupation authorities would have refused them the necessary recognition.[14]

It would not be until 1989, with the fall of the Berlin Wall, that the German Social Democratic Party could compete again in elections in the former Soviet zone of East Germany.

In Georgia in 1923, despite the forced self-dissolution of the Social Democratic Party, the compulsory resignation of many of its members, the arrests, the tortures, and the killings, the party survived. The formal dissolution of the party drove their organization further underground, where they continued to publish illegal newspapers, communicate with their leaders abroad, and prepare for armed insurrection against the hated Soviet regime.

Leaders of the Cheka in Georgia, among them Lavrenty Beria, were beginning to understand that the Georgian Social Democracy, with its decades-long history of struggle and its deep roots in the Georgian population, would not be so easy to kill off.

The national uprising against Soviet rule was now one year away.

PART II

Rebellion and Repression

CHAPTER 14

The Resistance

LENIN HAD BEEN ASSURED BY STALIN that a pro–Bolshevik uprising had occurred in Tiflis in 1921. As David Lang wrote, "According to Stalin and his man on the spot, Orjonikidze, the Mensheviks had already been virtually overthrown by the Georgian masses themselves, and the appearance of a few Red Army soldiers would simply consolidate a victory already won."[1]

But the truth eventually came out; Stalin and Orjonikidze had brazenly lied to the other Soviet leaders. Lenin and Trotsky, wrote Lang, were concerned about the reaction among foreign Socialists when they found out that "the Russian Communists were now overthrowing other, independent socialist régimes by force of arms."[2]

As we have seen, this is precisely what happened during the Berlin meeting the following year.

Stalin boasted about the impending conquest of Georgia months before it happened. In November 1920, he said that "Georgia, which has been transformed into the principal base of the imperialist operations of England and France and which therefore has entered into hostile relations with Soviet Russia, that Georgia is now living out the last days of her life."[3]

Lenin worried about the possibility of the Red Army invasion backfiring, prompting the kind of resistance that emerged. Early on, he wrote to Orjonikidze saying "I must remind you that the internal and international position of Georgia requires of the Georgian Communists not the application of the Russian stereotype, but ... an original tactic, based upon greater concessions to the petty bourgeois elements.."[4] But Orjonikidze wasn't listening.

The majority of Georgians did not welcome the Soviet invaders. Resistance began immediately, some of it peaceful. For example, the Social Democrat Kristine Sharashidze, one of a handful of female members of the Constituent Assembly of independent Georgia, organized a protest on February 25, 1922, as the new Communist rulers celebrated the first year of Soviet rule. Sharashidze was then teaching at the Tenth Pedagogical

Institute in Tiflis and several of her students joined in the protest. She was arrested but eventually freed.

Armed struggle also played a role almost from the beginning. Resistance was initially sporadic, disorganized, and ineffective.

That would change as the resistance learned from its mistakes and began to build coalitions, plan strategy, and tactics, and liaise with the Georgian government-in-exile, now based in France.

The Georgians had many reasons for their discontent with Soviet rule, as we have seen. These included the suppression of democracy, the banning of political parties, the suppression of a free press, the crushing of the independent trade unions, the Bolshevization of the cooperatives, and the war on the church. High unemployment, famine and a cholera outbreak also contributed to general discontent with the new regime.

Just a month after the departure of the Social Democratic government in 1921, a mass meeting took place in Tiflis' magnificent Opera House on Rustaveli Avenue. Some 3,000 representatives of workers' organizations took part. These were some of the people most likely to be open to cooperation with the new Soviet regime which now ruled in their name.

According to Soviet propaganda, the Georgian working class had been "liberated" from rule by the hated Social Democrats and their imperialist sponsors. However, the meeting did not proceed according to the Bolshevik script.

"It passed resolutions calling upon the *Revcom* [the Bolshevik government in the country] to defend Georgia's rights to self-determination and independence," wrote David Lang. In addition, the workers called on the new government "to hasten the formation of a national Red Army of Georgia; to secure for the working masses of Georgia the right to select their representatives by free elections; to ensure that the new Soviet order was introduced into Georgia in such a way as to respect the customs of the people; and to legalize the existence of all socialist organizations not actually engaging in activities directed against the régime."[5]

Lang wrote that these demands were "acceptable in the main to the local Georgian Bolsheviks" which shows how much the Georgian Soviet leadership was "infected" with nationalist ideas, even at this very early stage. In the years to come, there would be a major rift between those Georgian Bolsheviks who were inclined towards more self-determination and autonomy for the country and those, like Stalin and Orjonikidze, who treated their former homeland as a conquered Russian province.

The resolutions adopted at this meeting "were not in accordance with the policies of Stalin and his immediate associates," noted Lang. "Far from permitting the formation of a Georgian Red Army, Stalin saw that all military formations were disbanded, and posted Russian garrisons at strategic points." He was not going to trust the security of the new Soviet Georgia to Georgians.

The new regime was unpopular. Despite all the advantages one acquired from membership in the ruling Communist Party, Georgians did not flock to join its ranks. The Communists recruited perhaps 10,000 members—many times the size of their party before the Red Army's arrival, but still smaller than the Social Democrats.

On May 26, 1922, a year after the imposition of Soviet rule, protest demonstrations were held to mark the fourth anniversary of the foundation of the independent Georgian republic. Precautions taken by the Soviet regime to prevent these—including closing schools and posting Red Army troops in the streets of the capital—were ineffectual. Strikes broke out just before the anniversary. In Gori, railway workers encouraged a general strike.

As Donald Rayfield wrote:

> Church bells rang out; the republican anthem *Dideba* was played. The Cheka responded with live fire. In some areas, like Sukhumi, Russian soldiers refused to shoot. But demonstrations were dangerous: on the 1923 Independence Day, the underground Freedom Committee asked the public to stay indoors.[6]

Increasing repression by the Soviet regime ensured that this would not be repeated on future anniversaries.

In later years, Soviet historians accused the Georgian Social Democrats of hypocrisy, claiming that they publicly rejected armed struggle but were secretly preparing for a major national uprising all along. A half-century after the events described, I. Ia. Trifonov claimed that from the beginning, the Social Democrats preserved "their underground organizations" and "attempted subversive activity." The Social Democrats, he noted, were the most active of these underground political parties.

To be fair, the Social Democrats preserved their underground organizations because the Bolsheviks grew increasingly intolerant of them and every other non–Communist party. They could see from the experience of the Mensheviks in Russia that their party had only a limited amount of time left to operate in the open before it would be completely crushed.

And the Bolsheviks themselves, it should be recalled, not only maintained underground organizations during the years of tsarist rule but also in Georgia during the years of Social Democratic rule. The Social Democrats were right to maintain their underground organizations and to keep open the option of armed struggle.

The opponents of the new Soviet regime were "hiding behind the words of the slogan 'Through Democracy to Socialism,'" Trifonov wrote. And they dared to demand the holding of "free elections" (the quotation marks are from the original article) to be monitored by a "mixed committee of the three Internationals"—as was proposed at the Berlin conference in 1922. This showed that the meeting at the Reichstag was not entirely in vain, as it provided the Georgian Social Democrats with a rallying cry.

Not only were the Social Democrats and their allies raising demands for democracy and free elections—they also dared to call "the liberating march of the Red Army into Georgia an 'invasion by foreign troops,'" which, of course, it was. This was not the last time that Russian leaders would describe the arrival of Russian troops in another country as a "liberating march" even if the local population interpreted things differently. (The Russian invasion of Ukraine in 2022 was described by the Moscow government as an effort to rid Ukraine of its "Nazi" government, but strangely the Ukrainians did not welcome the Russian soldiers as liberators.)

The Social Democrats "intensified their anti–Soviet activity" in the summer and fall of 1922, according to Trifonov. In October of that year, the Social Democrats "submitted a petition to the Georgian Revolutionary Committee [the Revcom] with a demand for the proclamation of 'liberties' and the freeing of arrested counterrevolutionaries." In addition to the petition, the Social Democrats "soon provoked a strike at the Tiflis railway junction." This was certainly not a good omen, as the "workers' and peasants' government" of Soviet Georgia should have had the urban working class on its side, at least in Tiflis, eighteen months after the Bolshevik conquest of power in the country.

Trifonov wrote that this petition was an attempt to cover up the Social Democrats' real plan all along: an armed insurrection. Apparently, in a re-staging of Valiko Jugheli's bold raid on the Tiflis arsenal in 1917, the Social Democrats once again attacked according to the Soviet historian. "Having organized the stealing of munitions from the arsenal, they accelerated preparations for the revolt," he concluded.[7]

It did not take long for the first examples of armed resistance to Bolshevik rule to occur. Faced with an increasingly authoritarian regime, the Georgians had fewer and fewer legal and peaceful outlets for protest. Already in 1921, some of the defeated Georgian forces withdrew into the mountains and formed small partisan groups. Sporadic fighting continued in various parts of the country for several months.

Probably the most important example of this took place in western Georgia, in the highland province of Svaneti. A peasant rebellion broke out there in May 1921, just two months after the Russian victory. Armed groups led by Mosestro Dadeshkeliani, Nestor Gardapkhadze, and Bidzina Pirveli disarmed some units of the Red Army, expelled the local Soviet government, and blocked roads. The uprising spread south to Lechkumi. The rebels demanded the withdrawal of Red Army forces and the holding of free elections. They began preparations for a march on the city of Kutaisi.

In early October, the Communist government branded the rebels as "political bandits" and formed special military units to crush the revolt. According to Soviet reports, there were about 1,600 rebels and they were loyal to the National Democratic Party, though working together with the Tiflis-based Social Democrats. The Red Army forces managed to contain the rebellion in Svaneti, and by the end of the year, the revolt was over. Leading rebels were executed, and severe repression followed.

Long before preparations began for a nationwide uprising, small-scale insurgencies continued to take place against the Soviet occupiers. Some of those insurgencies were led by men who would play a key role in the 1924 uprising.

Early in 1922, a rebellion against the Soviets broke out in Khevsureti, a mountainous district in northeast Georgia. It was triggered by the new regime's war against the church. The revolt's leader was Kaikhosro (Kakutsa) Cholokashvili, a Georgian army officer and National Democrat who chose to remain behind when the Soviets invaded the country.

Kakutsa went to the Pankisi Valley in eastern Georgia and there formed the "Band of Sworn Men" which continued to fight the Bolsheviks.

"The biggest guerrilla detachment, which soon took on the aspect of a national army, was that led by" Kakutsa, according to a 1955 U.S. congressional report. "He and his gallant '*Shepitulis*' (sworn to die) soon became national heroes."[8]

Meanwhile, Kakutsa's men managed to take Manglisi, a small spa town not far from the capital, and raid Tiflis' suburbs. The Soviets hit back with airplanes and artillery and suppressed the uprising. Kakutsa crossed the border into Chechnya and from there launched raids into Georgia. Kakutsa initially led an independent group of armed men, but later agreed to take orders from the Damkom. He would play a key role in the 1924 rebellion.

In early 1923, rebels in Guria, the Social Democratic stronghold in western Georgia, killed three Soviet secret police. In response, the Soviets killed 92 men and promised to kill more if violence continued. By March 1924, Beria claimed that the country was "literally flooded with a network of criminal and political bands, dominated by the Mensheviks."[9]

However, these local rebellions in Svaneti and Khevsureti were small-scale affairs and posed no serious challenge to Soviet rule in Georgia. The majority of active partisan detachments had either disintegrated or surrendered to the Soviets by 1923.

Meanwhile, the leadership of the various Georgian political parties in exile united behind the Paris-based Social Democratic government headed by Noe Zhordania. This marked a significant shift, as the smaller opposition parties, including the National Democrats, had previously been quite critical of the majority Social Democrats. It took the Soviet invasion in 1921 to convince them all to work together to restore Georgian independence.

Some of the key commanders of the resistance forces would come from the National Democrats. But after the rebellion's defeat, hostility between the competing factions resumed—not least because they blamed each other for what happened.

In addition to unifying the various Georgian factions, the government-in-exile reached out to representatives of neighboring countries, including Armenia, with which Georgia had fought a brief war following independence in 1918. Zhordania and his comrades were keen to create a united front of all the nations that had recently been occupied by the Soviets, which had fallen one by one to Moscow's rule. Like the decision of all the non–Bolshevik parties to work together, this, too, was a lesson learned from the successful Soviet conquest of all the formerly independent South Caucasian states.

In early May 1922, little more than a year after the Soviets came to power in Georgia, all the non–Bolshevik political parties in the country formed *Damkom*—"The Committee for the Independence of Georgia."

The Georgian opposition had learned the lessons of the Red Army invasion in February 1921 and of the defeat of the Svanetian uprising later that year. It was time for coordinated, nationwide action to prepare for an armed revolt against Moscow's rule of the country.

In addition to the Social Democrats, who played the leading role, other parties joining Damkom included the National Democratic Party, the Socialist Federalist Party, the Social Revolutionaries, and the *Skhivi* ("Beam") Party, a dissident Social Democratic faction led by the former Minister of War, Grigol Giorgadze. Each party was given one seat on the committee, leading to the group also being known as the "Parity Committee."

Noe Zhordania, President of the Georgian Democratic Republic and leader of the Social Democratic Party (author's collection).

This time the National Democrats, Social Democrats, and others would unite against the Bolsheviks. The Social Democrats were prepared to concede something in the Damkom that had never been their policy when they ruled the country: a coalition including all the non–Communist parties. Before the Soviet invasion, there had been no need for such a coalition as free elections had shown the Social Democrats to be overwhelmingly popular. But faced with the national emergency of Soviet occupation, the Social Democrats were prepared to concede the need for alliances between previously hostile factions.

As the largest party, the Social Democrats provided a chairman for Damkom, the first of which was Gogita Paghava, who was succeeded by

Nikoloz Kartsivadze. Kartsivadze in turn was arrested by the Cheka on March 16, 1923, and was replaced with Prince Kote Andronikashvili. Damkom's Secretary was a leader of the National Democrats, Yason Javakhishvili. The Damkom kept in close contact with Zhordania and the rest of the Georgian government-in-exile through a bureau based in Istanbul.

Inside Georgia, Damkom set up a military command chaired by the retired general Kote Abkhazi. Abkhazi had served as a major general in command of artillery in the Russian army during the First World War. After the war, he was one of the founders of the National Democratic Party in Georgia and helped establish the new university in Tiflis. Like Kakutsa, he remained behind in Georgia when the Red Army took over the country and put himself at the disposal of the Damkom to lead its military operations.

Less than nine months after the Damkom was formed, its military center was dealt a severe blow by the Cheka, the Soviet secret police. They managed to infiltrate agents into the organization. One of them was a National Democrat student named Mesablishvili.

Mass arrests followed. Kote Abkhazi, along with 14 members of the Damkom's Military Center, was arrested in February 1923. The others were General Alexandre Andronikashvili, General Varden Tsulukidze, General Rostom Muskhelishvili, Colonel Elizbar Gulisashvili, Colonel Alexandre Machavariani, Colonel Gogi Khimshiashvili, Colonel Dimitri Chrdileli, Lieutenant Levan Klimiashvili, Captain Simon Bagration-Mukhraneli, Captain Ivane Karangozishvili, Lieutenant Parnaoz Karalashvili, Iason Kereselidze, Simon Chiabrishvili, Ivane Kutateladze, and Nikoloz Zanduk.

"The detainees were brutally tortured," it has been reported, "but none of them betrayed their comrades."[10]

Kote Abkhazi's last words before he was shot were: "I meet death happily, as through luck it has fallen to me to sacrifice myself for the cause of Georgia. My death will bring glory to Georgia!"[11]

The uprisings in Svaneti and Khevsureti had been crushed. Damkom's Military Center no longer existed. Kakutsa and his "Band of Sworn Men" were still around but were confined to raids from across the border. There was no sign of support for a rebellion from any foreign power and the new Soviet regimes in neighboring countries were not going away. Some leaders of the Damkom were convinced that the Georgian people were apathetic and not ready to join an uprising.

The timing of the uprising was important. It was originally supposed to take place on May 26, 1924, the sixth anniversary of the proclamation of Georgian independence. It was delayed in order to take advantage of the summer vacation of Red Army troops when fresh, untrained conscripts would be arriving. Mid–August was agreed as the new date, but that too was postponed due to the arrests of leading Social Democrats in Georgia.

But in the end, the leaders of the resistance decided to go ahead with their plans for a national uprising in Georgia at the end of August 1924.

CHAPTER 15

The Road to Rebellion

WHILE THE SOCIAL DEMOCRATS IN EXILE and underground in Georgia were making their plans to overthrow the Soviet regime, their enemies were working overtime to ensure that that would never happen.

The All-Russian Extraordinary Commission for Combating Counter-Revolution, Profiteering, and Corruption (the Cheka) fought against the enemies of Communist rule from the very start of Soviet power in Georgia, as they had been doing in Russia ever since Lenin ordered the creation of a secret police in December 1917.

Lenin named Felix Dzerzhinsky to head up the new organization which took on the role that had been performed by the Tsar's Department of Police (which together with other security services was collectively known as the Okhrana). The Cheka changed names repeatedly, but its function remained largely unchanged—it was the "sword and shield" of the Bolshevik regime.

The tools at its disposal varied during the different historic periods. In Lenin and Stalin's time, the Cheka could freely execute individuals and did so on an industrial scale. Following Stalin's death in 1953, the organization became somewhat less murderous—but was still responsible for the suppression of dissent and maintained a large network of prisons and labor camps. By 1995 it had been replaced by the Federal Security Service of the Russian Federation, known as the FSB. The FSB and other Russian security services are markedly less bloodthirsty than the Cheka's previous incarnations. But they remain much feared and secretive organizations that operate outside the law, both inside the Russian Federation and abroad.

The date on which the Cheka was founded, December 20, 1917, has been marked as a holiday in Russia ever since. President Vladimir Putin, himself a proud Chekist from his time in the KGB, has made a point of thanking all serving and former security service personnel on that day each year.

Following the Soviet invasion of Georgia in February 1921, a Georgian Cheka was established to ensure the security of the regime. As the opposition parties in Georgia geared up for a national uprising in August 1924, the Cheka's capacity to repel threats to the Soviet regime would be tested to the full.

One of the key elements in the Cheka's arsenal was something they inherited from their Okhrana predecessors—the strategy of *provokatsiia*. Provokatsiia was a true innovation in the tsarist regime's fight against an opposition that largely operated underground. Instead of merely trying to learn what opposition groups were up to and arresting their leaders, the police would instead recruit collaborators who were encouraged to rise in the ranks of their respective parties.

In some cases, most famously that of Ievno Azef, those agents rose to the very tops of their organizations and as part of their work for the police organized unsuccessful and also successful attacks, including on the imperial family. Azef, a long-term paid agent of the police, rose to head the feared Combat Organization of the Socialist Revolutionary Party and took charge of the organization's extensive terrorist operations—with the knowledge and support of his police handlers. Azef escaped revolutionary justice and died of natural causes in Berlin in 1918.

The strategy of provokatsiia was also applied successfully by the Okhrana in their fight against the Bolsheviks. Among the Okhrana's successes was their agent Roman Malinovsky, who rose to lead the Bolshevik faction in the Fourth State Duma, serving from November 1912 to May 1914. He was highly paid by the Okhrana and had been given the code name "*Portnoi*" (tailor). When Malinovsky was finally exposed as a police spy—and forced to flee Petrograd—Lenin angrily denied the accusation, until that position was no longer tenable. In 1918 Malinovsky found his way back to Russia after the Bolshevik seizure of power and was captured and shot.

As the tsarist police had done, the Cheka planted agents and informants inside all the opposition groups, both those that remained inside Soviet Russia and those who escaped into exile. The Cheka even created completely fake opposition groups to lure people identified as threats to the regime back to Soviet Russia—most famously in the case of "The Trust." This purported to be a powerful underground anti–Bolshevik group inside Russia.

The Cheka tried to stay one step ahead of the growing resistance in

Georgia as they had done in Russia. But just as there was a lack of loyal Communists in the country, there were not enough men to create a local version of the secret police. The Soviets brought in experienced men like Lavrenty Beria, who had been working in Baku. In Russia, with the civil war now over, skilled interrogators and paramilitary troops could be redeployed to Georgia.

The Chekists were quick to make mass arrests and carried out shootings of those deemed to be a threat to the new Communist regime in the country. Those executions were carried out without trials, and many took place in Vake, then an empty field in Tiflis (it would later become a park).

But their work did not always go smoothly. One problem was that there were two Chekas—a Georgian one and a Transcaucasian one. The Transcaucasian Cheka complained that the Georgian Cheka was arresting its informers. Some of the new Chekists were hardened criminals recently released from prison. They murdered and robbed Communists as well as aristocrats and others deemed hostile to the new regime. According to one account, by the end of 1923, the Cheka had "taken out" nearly 700 "bandits."[1]

Over time, the Cheka's grip in Georgia was tightening. As David Lang wrote:

> The Russian secret police brought with them their well-tried techniques of torture and intimidation, in which some of their local recruits proved very adept pupils. The Metekhi fortress jail, which had served the Tsars as a political prison, was crammed with captives, while the most obstinate cases were "worked over" in the dreaded Cheka headquarters down in the city, where hundreds of miserable prisoners languished and died in conditions of indescribable squalor.[2]

According to another account, the reception accorded to Stalin by the railway workers led the Cheka to focus attention on them as potential opponents of the regime. As Tadeusz Wittlin wrote in his biography of Beria, "several arrests had been made and there was no doubt about the hostile spirit prevailing among these workers. In the Tiflis railway plants, Beria had a few informers who reported signs of dissatisfaction and repeated to him critical comments and the names of the dissenters."[3]

But it was not only in Tiflis that reports of dissent and unrest were reaching the Cheka. "From his agents and investigators Beria received reports about a strong opposition movement in the longshoremen's communities in the harbour of Batumi," Wittlin wrote. "They also reported that in Kutaisi and Sukhumi there still existed organisations of the intelligentsia, Mensheviks, and officers of the former Georgian National Army, and that this independence movement was very active."[4]

The Georgian government-in-exile, led by Noe Zhordania, had decided to organize an armed uprising to overthrow Soviet rule.

On March 10, 1924, Zhordania wrote a letter to the Central Committee of the Georgian Social Democratic Party. He outlined a plan for a national uprising but was insistent that it must take place across the entire region and not only in Georgia. In an earlier message to Jugheli, back in December 1921, Zhordania made it clear that Georgia alone could not win a war against the Bolsheviks.

Zhordania was busy making friends among Georgia's neighbors who had also come under Soviet rule by early 1921. In June of that year, a declaration was published announcing that a union had been formed "to strengthen the independence, democracy and economic prosperity of the republics of the North Caucasus, Armenia, Azerbaijan and Georgia and to put an end to all confrontation among these republics and ... firmly establish solidarity."[5]

They were playing for the highest stakes and decided to infiltrate some of their very best people into Georgia. With the uprising scheduled to begin in the summer of 1924, the architect of the agrarian reform, former Agriculture Minister Noe Khomeriki, and the former head of the National Guard, Vladimir "Valiko" Jugheli, were smuggled into the country. This was possible because of relatively porous borders and an agreement with Turkey that people living near the border could come and go unhindered.

By 1924, Jugheli was 37 years old and a well-known figure in Georgia. As a very young Social Democrat, he initially sided with Lenin and the Bolsheviks when the Party split. But unlike Stalin and a few other Georgians, he did not stay long in the Bolshevik camp and eventually became a follower of Zhordania and the Social Democrats. But in this role, ruthlessly fighting the enemies of the Georgian Democratic Republic until 1921, there was more than the whiff of the Bolshevik in him.

Back in September 1917, before the Bolsheviks seized power in Petrograd before Georgia became independent, the Social Democrats in Tiflis organized a militia consisting of armed workers. It was known at first as the Workers' Guard or Red Guard. Jugheli was its leader. His men were fiercely loyal to the Social Democratic Party and would in time constitute a praetorian guard for the ruling party in the new Georgian state when it was created the following year.

The Workers' Guard was ruled by an elected congress, and its general staff was elected to a one-year term. When Georgia became an independent state, the Guard was under the direct control of the Social Democratic-dominated parliament rather than the Minister of War and was eventually renamed the National Guard.

Jugheli's first success, in the fall of 1917, was the stuff of legend. At the time, there were thousands of Russian troops still in Georgia, many of whom had Bolshevik sympathies. There were fears that they might attempt a military coup. To prevent this, and to ensure that the democratic forces in Georgia had a well-equipped military force of their own, Jugheli and his men raided the Tiflis arsenal and seized weapons.

So successful was this daring raid that for some years afterward December 12 was celebrated as a national holiday, second only to Independence Day on May 26. (It was known as the Day of the National Guard.) The raid on the arsenal is what ensured that Georgia did not immediately fall under Soviet Russian domination and instead went on to enjoy several years of freedom from Bolshevik rule.

Beria's son Sergo wrote a biography of his father painting him, unsurprisingly, in a favorable light. What he wrote must be treated as hearsay—at best. The Cheka, he said, had already learned a great deal about the impending uprising in 1924. "My father wanted to avoid a clash, to prevent a mass uprising and intervention by Russian troops," he wrote. "He feared the repression that would inevitably ensue."[6]

According to Sergo, his father sent a report to Orjonikidze, who headed up the Communist organization for all of Transcaucasia. Orjonikidze shared the report with Stalin. "Doubtless with Moscow's blessing," he wrote, Beria was authorized "to make contact with the Mensheviks. He was to let them know that their plan had been discovered and to dissuade them from going ahead with the adventure. The Mensheviks received this warning but, under pressure from the British, declared that it was a 'provocation.'"[7]

This reference to the British fits the Soviet narrative that the 1924 uprising was done at the behest of Western imperialist powers, though there is no evidence of this.

According to Sergo Beria, his father proposed to meet with one of the Social Democrats in Georgia. He "would prove that he knew where all their caches of arms were located. They sent the former commander of the Georgian Menshevik Guard, Jugeli, to him."[8]

Sergo Beria believed that Jugheli had been brought to Tiflis to meet the Cheka and was supposed to return to Kakhetia. But Jugheli "had found a mistress" and "abandoning all caution" he stayed in the Georgian capital. According to Sergo's account, one of Jugheli's former mistresses denounced him. And Beria's boss, Kvantaliani—who Sergo described as "an absolute imbecile"—boasted that he had captured the infamous head of the National Guard.

Jugheli was certain that he had been betrayed. He had not been in Tiflis for a long time, and very few people were aware that he had returned. He described his contacts as a "very limited circle." "It became obvious to me," he said, "that someone from this 'limited circle' turned me in."[9]

On the night of August 7–8, 1924, Jugheli was locked into a Cheka cell in Tiflis. He tried to take his own life, severing his veins. His jailers thwarted the attempt and saved his life—for a time. Only the Cheka would decide whether he lived or died.

According to Sergo, when his father heard about Jugheli's arrest, he rushed over to meet Orjonikidze. The Bolshevik leader—"for the first time"—disappointed the young Chekist. "I warned you," said Orjonikidze, "that if the affair became public I should not lift my little finger."[10]

There are different accounts of what happened next. It appears that Beria went looking for Jugheli in one of the Cheka's jails.

According to a recent Russian account, "Everything was done to make Valiko feel like a partner, not a prisoner. He was allowed to speak with other arrested Mensheviks, and wine was served at a generous table."[11]

Beria told Jugheli that the Cheka knew everything about their plans, and warned him that the uprising would end in disaster. This was the proposal made by the Cheka leaders to Jugheli: "The Mensheviks renounce the uprising, recognize Soviet power, in return a broad political amnesty is announced, and the Mensheviks are given posts in the government of Georgia."[12]

By August 12, Jugheli wrote letters to the Social Democratic Party's Central Committee and the Damkom. He urged them to call off the uprising, which had been compromised. The Cheka, it seemed, knew all about it. Jugheli told his comrades that the restoration of Georgian independence was now a pipe dream. And Georgia received certain benefits from being under the control of Soviet Russia. For example, he wrote, the country had more cultural and national autonomy than it had under the tsars.

But his comrades outside of prison understood correctly that he had written the letters under duress. As Timothy Blauvelt explained, "There is an undocumented story that instead of warning them off, Jugheli was actually conveying to the planners that the initial plan to start the uprising in the cities was blown and that they should enact a secondary plan to start the rebellion in the countryside."[13]

Jugheli concluded that the only way to stop an uprising that was guaranteed to end in a bloodbath was for him to meet the rebel leaders face-to-face. He asked the Cheka for permission to be released on a temporary basis. As a guarantee that he would return to their custody, he suggested that the Chekists give him a slow-acting poison. But to no avail—he was not released.

On August 26, Jugheli's letters were published in Georgian and Russian in local newspapers. The letters stunned the nation. The leader of the uprising was calling for its cancellation. Other letters by other opposition leaders recanting their fight against the Bolsheviks were also published at the same time.

One of these was by the former Russian Socialist Revolutionary Boris Savinkov, a legendary terrorist (and novelist) who had clandestinely returned to Russia to meet up with the fake "Trust" organization. Savinkov, like Jugheli, was captured in August 1924 and seemingly wrote a letter rejecting his long-held anti–Bolshevik views.

The Cheka had hit upon an effective strategy to decapitate anti–Communist movements and applied it successfully in the cases of both Jugheli and Savinkov.

Lavrenty Beria, meanwhile, apparently wrote to Orjonikidze and Cheka boss Dzerzhinsky telling them that he disagreed with the handling of Jugheli. He requested leave to join his pregnant wife for a time. He was at last granted his request, at the end of August, to visit her in the village of Abastuman. He arrived on August 21.

The national uprising was now one week away.

CHAPTER 16

Chiatura

DESPITE THE ARRESTS OF THE MEMBERS OF Damkom's Military Committee, despite the capture of the prominent Social Democratic leaders who
had arrived from abroad, and despite the fact that the Cheka had obviously
penetrated the resistance and was aware of their plans, the long-planned
insurrection went ahead at 04:00 on Thursday, August 28, 1924.

The Social Democrats felt that the uprising had to go ahead, despite
the setbacks, for several reasons. One of these, perhaps the most important, was that several European countries (including Britain) were in the
process of "normalizing" relations with Soviet Russia. This included not
only diplomatic recognition but also trade relations. If the Georgians
delayed any longer, they could no longer count on any kind of foreign support. Though as we shall see, it may already have been too late.

There may also have been a sense in which the uprising would go
ahead even if it faced certain defeat. In some ways, it could be compared to
the 1916 Easter Rebellion in Ireland. As Timothy Blauvelt wrote, the Georgian uprising of 1924 "bears a striking similarity to the conception of 'winning by losing' associated with the 1916 Easter Rising in Ireland, although
there are no indications in any of the sources related to Georgia that any of
the actors drew such a comparison at the time."[1]

The rebels at that time would have insisted that the uprising did stand
a chance of winning, and they were seeking victory—not martyrdom.

The uprising began in Chiatura, the center of the Georgian manganese mining region. Manganese, Georgia's most important export, is a
critical ingredient in the production of steel and other alloys.

As described by a Soviet historian writing many years later, "the
numerically small bands of rebels took by surprise the sleeping population
of the town." He claimed that only about thirty people were involved in the
rebellion, and they were all "Mensheviks, noblemen, and tsarist officers."
According to the official Soviet explanation, to these rebels were added
several unemployed workers who had been bribed to join the uprising.[2]

In Orjonikidze's report to Moscow, he wrote that "the signal for a general uprising was the seizure of Tchiatura and Sachkhere stations by armed detachments, carried out on August 28, 1924, at 4 o'clock in the morning."[3]

This was a day earlier than planned, according to most historical accounts. No one knows exactly why the rebellion started when it did.

Donald Rayfield added some details to Orjonikidze's account. "112 socialist federalist fighters with one machine gun (which jammed) took the railway station and bridges, arresting or killing communist officials. Over a thousand rebels, from peasants to schoolteachers, then attacked villages around Kutaisi."[4]

Soviet historians claimed that the rebels first arrested the Communists, Soviet government officials, and trade union personnel in the town and that they promptly established a "provisional government" headed up by one "Prince Tsereteli." The new government proclaimed a state of siege and issued an appeal to the population. "The appeal contained slander against the communists and false assertions that 'all of Georgia had risen, the entire Transcaucasia, the Caucasus, and all parts of Russia will rise in their wake.'"[5]

All of Georgia had not risen, nor would it. If this is what the insurgents were saying, they were being overly optimistic.

If the rebels were attempting to rally broad public support for their campaign, according to Soviet historians they went about this in a very strange way. Instead of concealing their unpopular reactionary agenda, they began to immediately implement it in broad daylight. "The manganese mine owners immediately returned to Chiatury [sic] in an attempt to regain the mines that had been confiscated from them," wrote Trifonov. "In the village of Chala ... [they] took land away from the peasants. In another village the nobility set about collecting corn from the peasants' fields."[6]

If this was the case, it explains the very rapid collapse of the rebellion in the town where it all began. The privatization of the mines and the seizing of corn from peasants would seem to be rather ineffective ways to win hearts and minds for the rebellion.

"In many places the rebels were routed by the volunteer detachments within a few hours," wrote Trifonov.

The communists in the town of Chiatury were able, before being arrested, to establish telegraphic contact with the town of Shorapany. At 8 a.m. on the morning of August 29, a small detachment of communards from Adzharia entered Chiatury without firing a shot. Fifty armed communists and a number of Cheka men from Shorapany participated actively in the liberation of the city. The peasants of Chiatury district forthrightly resisted being drafted and refused to support the rebels. The "provisional government" of Prince Tsereteli, which existed altogether for twenty-four hours, vanished in an unknown direction to save itself from the people's wrath. The peasants themselves arrested the rebels and demanded drastic punishment for them.[7]

In Orjonikidze's report to Stalin, he concluded this story, writing: "True, already on August 30 they were repulsed by the authorities. The rebels retreated into the mountains in the direction of Surami (a small town)."[8]

In other words, it seemed to be a poorly planned and poorly executed rebellion—a complete debacle, even if not exactly as the Soviet historians would later describe it.

Accounts of what happened on that first day in Chiatura vary widely. In an unreliable biography of Beria, we learn that "one of the coal mines at Chiaturi [*sic*] had been blown up with dynamite. This was the signal for the general outbreak of the insurrection to the Liberation Forces in western Georgia. Hundreds of miners and workers armed themselves not only with machine guns, rifles and bayonets, but also with lances and sabers used by the national cavalry, long Georgian daggers, or simply heavy pitchforks."[9]

A more recent account by one of Georgia's best-known writers today, Aka Morchiladze, has a slightly different version of the beginning of the rebellion in Chiatura. Most historians agree that the rebellion in Chiatura was premature, with different explanations of why this happened. According to Morchiladze, "the attack began 24 hours early because the revolutionary fighters, then hiding in and around the streets, heard gunshots. Thinking this the opening act of the rebellion, they launched their own premature attack—which failed gloriously."[10]

Morchiladze writes that "the shooting came from a robbery of the local manganese mine office, carried out by some young, non-political opportunists, intending to time their theft with the chaos of the rebellion." They knew this, of course, because everyone did. The August uprising was the worst-kept secret in Georgian history. But the robbers, like the revolutionaries, got the date wrong.

It was not a brilliant beginning to the long-awaited national uprising against Soviet rule.

CHAPTER 17

The Uprising Spreads

THE UPRISING WAS OVER ALMOST AS SOON AS IT BEGAN.

The crushing of the revolt in Chiatura was not the end of the rebellion. Orjonikidze wrote that on the morning of the second day, the rebels began destroying telegraph wires that ran alongside the railway, as well as seizing railway stations all the way to Batumi.

Within a day of Orjonikidze's message reaching Moscow, *The New York Times* published what was probably the first news to reach the outside world about what was happening in Georgia. And it was practically a verbatim account of the Soviet state's propaganda. The story was entitled "SOVIET QUELLS REVOLT—Rising in Georgian Republic Lasts Only One Day" and it came from a Times reporter in Moscow. The article began by quoting the Soviet line: "An official statement by the Council of Commissars of the Georgian Republic announces the suppression of an attempt at a counterrevolutionary rising which aimed to overthrow the Soviet regime in Georgia."

The Times reported that "the rebels, composed of former officers, landowners and tradesmen, seized the town of Tshiatoury (Chiatura), in the Kutaisi district in the early hours of Friday, and succeeded in holding the town all day, but were driven out by Government forces with heavy losses. At other places, small villages, the rebels were still less successful. Their leaders were arrested."

"The rising is ascribed to the Central Committee of the Social Democrats and the committee of Nationalists headed by Prince Andronnikoff."[1]

There are some interesting things about this short article—not least the fact that it uncritically repeated an official Soviet report. It said that the rebellion barely lasted a day, when as we know it lasted for at least several more days and spread to other parts of the country. And more important, it labeled the rebels as "former officers, landowners and tradesmen"—in other words, the traditional enemies of the Bolshevik regime dating back to the Civil War. Not the miners, workers, peasants, fishermen, and school children armed with pitchforks reported in other accounts.

On the face of it, this characterization of the rebels made no sense. One of the greatest achievements of the short-lived independent Georgian Republic was the land reform. So popular was that reform that there was hardly any resistance to it from landlords (unlike what had happened in Russia). Why would the Social Democrats then organize a revolt of landowners?

This Bolshevik view of the rebels as landlords, capitalists, priests, and other reactionaries persisted for decades to come. A later Soviet account would refer to the 1924 uprising as a "Menshevik-Kulak revolt." (Kulak was a term used by the Communists to refer to wealthy peasants.)

The first cipher messages sent by Georgian Communist officials told a different story of both spreading unrest and successful countermeasures:

The authorities took vigorous action. So, in Batumi, a combat detachment of Georgian Mensheviks led by a military troika was arrested. At the same time, from Tiflis and Batumi, under the cover of an armored train, detachments of Red Army soldiers and employees of the transport Cheka began to oust the rebels from the railway tracks. By August 31, the path from Samtredia to Batumi was cleared, and by September 1, the destruction in the railroad strip was corrected. The rebels were driven out of the Kvaloni station, and an attempt to capture the city of Ozurgeti by the Mensheviks was prevented.[2]

The one-day revolt reported by *The New York Times* had turned out to be somewhat more substantial, widespread, and threatening to the Communist regime. For the most part, the fighting was contained in the western part of Georgia at first. As internal Soviet accounts reported:

On the Kutaisi-Tiflis line, on the night of September 1, the rebels managed to damage the telegraph wires on the Sagarejo-Badiauri stretch. At the same time, they failed in a timid attempt to capture Ior. On August 30, in the northwestern part of Georgia, the rebels captured the city of Zugdidi. It was soon recaptured by the Soviet units, but the withdrawn rebel forces joined with the rebels thrown back from the railroad strip, who began to threaten the city of Sukhumi-Kale in Abkhazia. At the same time, on August 30, the uprising engulfed Upper and Lower Svaneti, from where the rebellious detachments under the command of the former colonel Dadeshkeliani began to advance towards Kutaisi and Abkhazia. As a result, the connection between Sukhumi and Tiflis was interrupted, but remained with Rostov-on-Don.[3]

The fighting grew more intense and even involved a ship of the Soviet navy as fierce battles continued:

On September 2, the rebels managed to push back the Soviet detachment that had left Sukhumi, and they continued to hold the section of the road they had captured. A destroyer was urgently sent from Sevastopol to Sukhumi to help the authorities.[4]

But help was on its way also from Abkhazia, a region of Georgia that had early on fallen under Russian influence and that even today is occupied by the Russian army. Back in 1924, the Abkhazians came to the aid of the embattled Soviet forces. As the Soviet historian Trifonov later wrote:

> In all uczds of Abkhazia the peasants, under the leadership of the communists, established volunteer detachments and directed them against the rebels. Some villages provided as many as 300 volunteers. The Abkhazian detachments, headed by N. Lakoba, chairman of the republic's Council of People's Commissars, helped to rout the rebels in Ozurgety and Zugdidy uezds.[5]

After helping Beria secure Communist rule in Georgia, Nestor Lakoba went on to be the unchallenged ruler of Abkhazia for many more years. But according to some reports, in the end, he was murdered by Beria—who poisoned him.[6]

The Abkhazians were not unique. "The insurgency did not spread to the non–Georgian ethnic communities within Georgia, let alone to Azerbaijan or to the mountaineers or Cossaks of the north Caucasus," wrote Timothy Blauvelt.[7]

In Svaneti, in north-western Georgia, the rebellion failed to gain traction, despite the region having been in the past a hotbed of anti–Soviet partisan warfare. According to the Soviet account:

> Due to the hostile attitude of the population, especially the Svans, who feared for the loss of their pastures, the rebel movement in this region began to wane, and they began to scatter to neighbouring areas. In this situation, the authorities of Soviet Georgia faced the problem of infiltration of certain groups of rebels into other regions and took measures to prevent them from entering Svaneti, Karachai and Balkaria.[8]

The rebels had some successes in western Georgia. As Wittlin wrote:

> Despite its start, which was not in accordance with the plan, the insurrection became too widespread to be easily smothered by the Soviet invaders. During the first week of hostilities, the patriots seemed to be victorious. But their equipment and supplies soon became inadequate.[9]

The uprising was limited to only certain parts of the country:

Of the 18 uezds in Georgia the revolt embraced one in its entirety and parts of four. In five communities of Tiflis Uezd about 30 persons joined the rebels. The anti–Soviet action gained significant scope only in Guria, where the kulak and prosperous strata of the villages participated. However, even in the very largest centres of the revolt, the plotters found not more than 150–200 persons on their side.[10]

In a Cold War–era U.S. Congressional report, the rebels were portrayed in an entirely different light. "Communist officials were captured and thrown into prison," the report declared. But Damkom had given "strict orders that none of the captured Communists were to be executed. They were to be tried later according to the laws of the Georgian Republic."[11]

Soviet historians disputed that description of the behavior of the insurgents. But Karl Kautsky, writing in 1924, confirmed the essential truth of that report. He wrote:

> What an abyss separates these people [the Bolsheviks] from us—[here is] just one example from the recent past. During the last uprising against the Bolshevik yoke in Georgia in September of this year, the insurgents managed to capture a number of outstanding Communists. Kakhiani, one of the leading Communists in Georgia, reported on their fate at a meeting of the Georgian Communist Party in Tiflis.[12]

Kautsky quoted Kakhiani's statement as it appeared in the official newspaper of the Communist Party on September 11, shortly after the suppression of the uprising:

> We have not made any announcement (about the fate of the prisoners) so far, either in the press or in meetings, because we knew they would return safe and sound. We were sure that these people (the insurgent Mensheviks) would not dare to harm them. In fact, the Mensheviks proved to be weak, cowardly and soft-hearted in this respect.[13]

The Bolsheviks would never be accused by anyone of being "weak, cowardly and soft-hearted." As Kakhiani wrote: "They would not execute any of our comrades, although we shot hundreds of them, even members of their Central Committee."[14]

As Kautsky summed it up, "For the magnanimous humanity of his opponents he has only scorn."[15]

According to more recent Soviet accounts, the collapse of the rebellion was due to the counter-productive and reactionary policies of the

Social Democrats. Here is how Trifonov described what happened to towns taken by the rebels:

> In the occupied towns and villages the rebels reinstituted the *zemstvos* [local governments], proclaimed the return of the nationalized lands to the land-owners and buildings to merchants, conducted prayer services, and published proclamations with boastful communiques. They arrested communists and their families.[16]

Donald Rayfield offers this account of how it all ended:

> Within three days, the rebellion was put down; aircraft dropped leaflets promising "forgiveness" for surrender. Menshevik hostages were shot somewhere between Moscow and Rostov. Imeretian rebels were packed into six railway carriages, which stopped outside Zestaponi, where graves were dug; 96 men were shot with Mauser pistols, others machine-gunned; the bodies were covered with quicklime. Five hundred Mingrelian rebels were shot in Senaki.[17]

One of the areas of Georgia where the uprising did not take hold was the capital, Tiflis. According to Soviet reports, "In the capital of Georgia itself, the tense situation continued, since, according to the information available to the Cheka, the rebels were expected to act by September 1."[18]

The expected attack did not come. But there were concerning incidents:

> From the moment of the uprising of the Georgian Mensheviks, the connection of Tiflis with Vladikavkaz, Sukhumi and other cities of the republic was repeatedly interrupted. There was a small armed conflict with the command staff of the local artillery battalion and [Socialist] federalist students who were preparing for an uprising.[19]
> The initial response of the Soviet forces was to flee. In a suburb of Tiflis the Soviet troops, attacked by the patriots, fled from their quarters and left the town. The partisans barricaded themselves and shot mortars, machine guns and light cannons; single snipers were firing from the tops of the trees.[20]

In the area around Tiflis, a major role was assigned to the Georgian soldiers serving in the Red Army. Trifonov mentioned that the formation of Georgian units was enormously important and that Lenin had written to Orjonikidze a year after the invasion of Georgia urging that such units be established.[21]

The formation of Georgian national units in the Red Army had been a demand of protesting workers as early as 1921—a demand which was emphatically rejected at the time by Stalin and Orjonikidze.

Meanwhile, in eastern Georgia, a force of rebels headed by the charismatic former army officer Kakutsa Cholokashvili had been waiting impatiently to attack.

One eyewitness, Alexander Sulkhanishvili, was serving with Kakutsa's men. He recalled that "On the morning of the twenty-ninth of August, one of our allies rushed to us and brought us the news that an uprising had begun in Chiatura the day before. That same morning, on August 29, the government began arresting and shooting suspects throughout eastern Georgia, particularly in Kakheti. These conditions completely emptied the foundation of a well-organized organizational scheme in Kakheti. But the Soviets were ready, and the capital Tbilisi was occupied by large security forces and would not be taken."[22]

In addition to being under the full military control of the Red Army and Cheka, the local population in Tiflis seemed skeptical of the rebels' claims that the uprising was occurring across Transcaucasia and that Georgia could count on British support.

Internal Soviet messages reported widespread support for the Communist regime, which had been in power for more than three years. "Today in Tiflis the workers demonstrated against the Mensheviks and their solidarity with the Soviet authorities," one message declared. "The demonstration was impressive: about 25 thousand workers took part in it, and the railway workshops—to the last man."[23]

The official Soviet line was that the Communist Party successfully led the enraged masses against the "Menshevik bandits." Here is how a Soviet historian described the suppression of the uprising:

> The Menshevik adventure caused an outburst of outrage among the working class, the toiling peasants, and the bulk of the intelligentsia. The rebels found themselves in total ideological and political isolation. The population of Georgia, including a considerable portion of the former Mensheviks, actively supported Soviet power. Volunteer detachments for struggle against the rebels were established in Tiflis, Kutaisi, and other cities. In Abkhazia, Adzharia, Chorokh, and other uezds, large detachments of peasants were organized. The Communist Party members and Komsomols were the cement that held the volunteer detachments together. The Georgian units of the Red Army conducted themselves superbly in the battles against the rebels. The suppression of the revolt was led directly by prominent figures in the Communist Party: G.K. Ordzhonikidze, M.G. Tskhakaia, F.E. Makharadze, and M.D. Orakhelashvili.[24]

As a message from the local Communist leadership to Stalin made clear on September 2, even Kakutsa's forces were no match for the Soviet army and Cheka. The rebel "gang," it reported, was "pursued by us—50 people, today at five and a half hours made a raid on Dusheti, but having met a swift blow from local communards, at seven and a half hours they were knocked out and disappeared in a northeast direction from Dusheti (District). The gang is pursued by our cavalry."[25]

The national rebellion came to an end with the arrest of its leaders at the Shio-Mghvime Monastery near the town of Mtskheta, just north of Tiflis. Damkom chairman Konstantine (Kote) Andronikashvili was a 48-year-old Social Democrat and a member of the Constituent Assembly of the independent Georgian Republic. Yason Javakhishvili, a National Democrat, was the Secretary of the Damkom. Among other Damkom leaders arrested were Ishkhneli, Jinoria, and Bochorishvili. Following the arrests, Beria met with several members of the Damkom. He made them an offer that they could not refuse. This is what Beria told the defeated Georgian leaders:

> You are defeated, but the fighting continues here and there. We will certainly be able to exterminate these detachments, but it will entail shedding blood in vain. You, the committee, are able to stop these armed detachments; make a declaration urging these isolated detachments to put down their arms and on our side, we will not harm them and we will stop all arrests and mass executions.[26]

They accepted the proposal with one condition: Beria must give the order to stop the executions. According to one account, the Chekist replied: "If the committee agrees, at the very instant the declaration is published the government will give the order everywhere, by direct line, to stop the executions."[27]

The Damkom members asked if Beria's proposal needed to be approved by the Soviet Georgian government. "Whatever is decided in this office," he told them "is at the same time the government's decision."[28]

The Damkom leaders were forced to sign a declaration that went beyond a simple call for the rebels to down their weapons. It made them denounce the uprising itself as "an adventure carried out by the upper classes."[29] Donald Rayfield added that "Kote Andronikashvili was even allowed a final word, claiming a moral victory for the uprising."[30]

As we shall see, this was not the last time that Georgians spoke about the "moral victory" they had won in 1924. Noe Zhordania returned to this idea in his analysis of what had happened.

As Amy Knight wrote:

Having extorted this damning document from the committee leaders, Cheka officials had it published immediately, both at home and in the foreign press. They then proceeded with mass arrests and executions in flagrant violation of the agreement made by Beria with rebel leaders. The Bolsheviks retaliated against their erstwhile opponents with extreme ferocity. Armed detachments, composed of army and Cheka troops, raided villages and killed entire families.[31]

In a later trial against the Damkom leaders, the Communist government released details of a Cheka investigation. The Damkom, unsurprisingly, was accused of ties to "the Mensheviks to other counterrevolutionary parties, White emigrés, and the Second International, as well as the launching of political bandit raids and the preparation for the revolt."[32]

The fighting was over, but the terror had just begun.

CHAPTER 18

Panic in Moscow

THREE AND A HALF YEARS AFTER the successful overthrow of the Social Democratic government in Tiflis, the man who boasted to Moscow that the red flag was now flying over the Georgian capital, Sergo Orjonikidze, panicked.

Two days after the revolt in Chiatura broke out, Orjonikidze sent an encrypted message to Moscow addressed to Stalin. Orjonikidze also copied in Mikhail Vasilyevich Frunze, a celebrated leader of the Red Army during the Civil War, and Vyacheslav Menzhinsky. Menzhinsky was a leading figure in the Cheka and its eventual head following the death of the organization's founder, Felix Dzerzhinsky, in 1926.

By this time, the rebels in Chiatura had already been routed. There were no reports of foreign military intervention in support of the uprising. And yet Orjonikidze reported that the whole country was in the grip of an uprising.

"Yesterday at dawn, a band of several dozen people attacked Chiatura and occupied it, disarming our people," he wrote. "Early this morning, the gang was driven out of the city." Despite that early success, the insurrection was spreading. "Today, almost all over Georgia [there are] actions of individual groups of the former People's Guards and Mensheviks, who are intensively preparing for an attack on Tiflis."[1]

There was more than a hint of fear in the tone of this message. But there was also something missing: there was no mention of kulaks (wealthy farmers), aristocrats, or other reactionary elements. There were no White army officers and no British or French imperialists. This would eventually change, but at the outset of the uprising, Orjonikidze correctly pointed the finger directly at supporters of the former Social Democratic government of independent Georgia, including the People's Guard that Valiko Jugheli had founded and led.

Orjonikidze's report to Moscow was based on first-hand knowledge. He participated in a high-level delegation of Bolsheviks to the Georgian towns of Senaki, Zugdidi, Shorapani, Kutaisi, and Ozurgeti. Georgian Party First Secretary Mikheil Kakhiani and Georgian Presidium members Mikha Tskhakaia, Fillip Makharadze, and Mamia Orekhelashvili accompanied Orjonikidze.

Stalin need not worry, Orjonikidze assured him, despite his reports of insurrection "almost all over Georgia." "Elimination measures have been taken," he told his boss. "More details tomorrow."[2]

But Stalin did need to worry. The uprising was on a "much larger scale than appeared in the Soviet newspapers, spreading to almost all regions of western Georgia," writes Giorgi Chkadua. The rebels "managed to seize the weapons depot" in Chiatura, "acquiring up to 200 rifles and bombs ... more than 10,000 people fought" in two districts. He concludes that the "severity of the subsequent repressions also validates the significance of the uprising."[3]

According to another report from 1955, based in part on eyewitness testimonies, "At first the insurrection was successful. Except in large towns, the Communists' resistance proved much weaker than expected."[4]

Later, Soviet historians challenged these accounts, claiming that the August revolt involved very small numbers of participants. "The attack on Chiatury [sic] was made by about 30 persons—Mensheviks, noblemen, and tsarist officers. About 50 unemployed they had bribed joined them. In five communities of Tiflis Uezd, about 30 persons joined the rebels."[5]

As one Soviet historian wrote, "By September 3 the rebellion was essentially put down."[6]

There was no uprising "almost all over Georgia." No one was "intensively preparing for an attack on Tiflis," as Orjonikidze had reported to Stalin. Months later, Stalin and other Communist leaders still spoke of the August 1924 uprising as if it had posed an existential threat to the Soviet regime. Even Trotsky referred to it as a "broad mass insurrection."[7]

It was not only Communist leaders in the Soviet Union who spoke this way about what had taken place in the late summer of 1924. Ruth Fischer, one of the leaders of the German Communist Party (KPD), wrote that "the series of peasant revolts [which] reached a peak in 1924 in the Georgian uprising ... was more nearly a civil war than the abortive Hamburg rising a year earlier."[8] The disastrous Hamburg rising had been organized by the KPD.

In a speech delivered on October 22, 1924, several weeks after the suppression of the uprising, Stalin showed signs of still being shaken by what had happened. "What happened in Georgia may be repeated all over Russia," he warned.[9]

Stalin appeared to believe Orjonikidze's initial description of a revolt across the country, threatening the survival of the Soviet regime. Instead of putting the uprising in perspective, noting how quickly it was suppressed and how little public support it had garnered (thanks to the work of the Cheka in the preceding months), Stalin saw more profound meaning in what had happened. Indeed, he thought there were lessons not only for the Georgian Soviet leadership but for the entire country.

Stalin said that the local Bolsheviks had grown complacent. "Our newspapers write that the events in Georgia were stage-managed," he said. "That is true, for, in general, the revolt in Georgia was an artificial, not a popular revolt…. In some places, thanks to the bad link between the Communist Party and the masses, the Mensheviks succeeded in drawing a section of the peasant masses into the revolt," he admitted.

The reference to "a section of the peasant masses" is interesting and echoes Ruth Fischer's description of the uprising as a "peasant revolt." Later Soviet historians would emphasize the role of kulaks, the nobility, and other elements—denying that any actual workers or peasants were involved.

And then Stalin dropped a bombshell. Referring to places where the uprising had shown some strength, he said that "it is characteristic that *they are the localities that are the most saturated with communist forces*…. And yet it was there that our people missed, overlooked, failed to notice the fact that there was unrest among the peasants, that something was brewing among them, that there was discontent among them, that it had been growing day by day, and the Party knew nothing about it. In the places most saturated with Communists, the latter proved to be most divorced from the sentiments, thoughts and aspirations of the non–Party peasantry."

Not a word about kulaks, nobles, or capitalists, nor even the usual accusation of foreign intervention. The problem was that the local Communists in Georgia, leaders of a "workers and peasants government," were "divorced" from the actual workers and peasants.

"That," he said, "is the crux of the problem." And though the uprising had failed in Georgia, the problem was not limited to that small country on the southern border of the Soviet Union. "The events in Georgia must be regarded as symptomatic," Stalin said. But symptomatic of what?

"What happened in Georgia may be repeated all over Russia if we do not radically change our very approach to the peasantry, if we do not create an atmosphere of complete confidence between the Party and the non–Party people if we do not heed the voice of the non–Party people, and, lastly, if we do not revitalise the Soviets in order to provide an outlet for the political activity of the toiling masses of the peasantry," he said.

The reference to "revitalizing" the Soviets is entirely disingenuous. In the early days of the Russian Revolution in 1917, soviets (councils) were created by industrial workers, soldiers, sailors, and peasants. In many cases, they were examples of direct democracy, with participation from all the left parties and not only the Bolsheviks.

But from the moment the Bolsheviks seized power in November of that year, the role of the soviets began to decline. Over the next several years, when free and fair elections to the soviets were held, opposition parties, including the Mensheviks, did very well. As a result, the elections were stopped, and the soviets drained of all their energy and importance. Stalin demanded that they be "revitalized," at least in Georgia, but he meant something else, as we shall see.

Stalin concluded his speech with this warning to Communists all over the country, not only in Georgia. "One thing or the other," he said. "Either we succeed in adopting the correct Leninist approach to the non–Party peasants in order to direct the growing political activity of the peasantry into the channel of constructive Soviet work and thus ensure that the peasants are led by the workers, or we fail to do this, in which case the political activity of the masses will by-pass the Soviets, will pass over the heads of the Soviets, and take the form of bandit revolts like that which occurred in Georgia."

It's worth pondering that formulation because this is not how future Soviet historians would characterize the 1924 revolt in Georgia. Stalin said that "the political activity of the masses will ... take the form of bandit revolts." In other words, these revolts involved not just a tiny minority of Mensheviks, directed by foreign imperialists, as would later be claimed, but were a kind of "political activity of the masses."

Stalin later wrote that if the Communists did not learn the correct lessons, "a new Tambov or a new Kronstadt are not in the least excluded" following the uprising in Georgia.[10]

Stalin was not the only Bolshevik leader to draw a comparison to the revolts in Kronstadt and Tambov. Grigory Zinoviev, who later became one of Stalin's main rivals, was the head of the Communist International in 1924. One of a handful of Lenin's most trusted deputies, Zinoviev also headed up the powerful Communist Party organization in Leningrad. In 1925 he, too, compared the Georgian uprising with the Kronstadt and Tambov revolts.[11]

A century ago, memories of the Kronstadt and Tambov revolts were fresh in the minds of the leaders of the Russian Communist Party. When Stalin or Zinoviev mentioned those revolts, everyone understood. The clear message was that the Georgian uprising of August 1924, though quickly suppressed by the Soviets, had posed an existential threat to the regime.

The Kronstadt revolt of March 1921 occurred while the Red Army was completing its conquest of Georgia. The Russian Civil War was effectively over, with the White armies, which had once threatened Moscow, now completely defeated. But discontent was rising in Petrograd, where the revolution had begun four years earlier, with increasing support for opposition parties. Splits were also emerging in the ruling Communist Party—which tolerated dissident factions, though that would soon end.

The sailors mutinied in the naval fortress of Kronstadt, located on an island just off the coast of Petrograd. Soviet propagandists would later label this a "White Guard" mutiny led by nobles, foreign imperialists, and the like. They made the same accusations about the 1924 uprising in Georgia three years later. However, the Bolshevik leaders were well aware that this was not the case.

"Red Kronstadt" had been critical to the success of Lenin's November 1917 coup d'état. The sailors had proven to be among the most militant opponents of the old regime and the most loyal to the new one. Yet by 1921, they had grown tired of empty Bolshevik promises and wanted the kind of society Lenin and his comrades had initially promised. They demanded a restoration of "soviet democracy" and indeed called for "soviets without Communists."

In their initial list of demands, the first three give a flavor of what the revolutionary sailors of Kronstadt wanted: new elections to the Soviets (which, they said, "do not express the will of the workers and peasants"); freedom of speech for workers and peasants—including for anarchists and left Socialist parties; and finally, "freedom of assembly for labor unions and peasant organizations." The demands resonated far beyond the naval fortress, and after failed attempts by Soviet officials to negotiate a way out of the crisis, the Bolsheviks decided to use force.

The Kronstadt mutiny was suppressed at the cost of thousands of lives, and though the Communist victory was complete, what happened at the naval fortress no doubt kept Stalin and other Bolshevik leaders awake at night.

In August 1920, months before the outbreak of the mutiny at Kronstadt, an incident took place in a village near the city of Tambov, 350 kilometers southeast of Moscow. According to Richard Pipes, a village "refused to surrender grain to a requisition team, killed several of its members, and fought off reinforcements."[12]

This was a fairly common event in Soviet Russia at this time. Lenin's policy of "war communism" meant that peasants were being squeezed to feed the urban working class, and armed units of workers were dispatched to the countryside to seize grain and other agricultural products. Independent Georgia had followed a different course, offering a comprehensive agrarian reform that turned peasants into loyal government supporters and ensured regular food supplies throughout the country.

"In 1918–1920," Pipes explained, "Tambov experienced the full brunt of forcible food exactions."[13]

The Bolshevik army commander leading the fight against the Tambov rebels was Vladimir Antonov-Ovseenko, who famously led the storming of the Winter Palace in Petrograd during the Bolshevik seizure of power in November 1917.

He described the causes behind Tambov's outbreak of "banditry." "The requisition assessment for 1920–1921, though reduced by half as against that of a year before, proved to be entirely excessive," he wrote. "With huge areas unsown and an exceedingly poor harvest, a considerable part of the province lacked enough bread to feed itself … half the peasantry was starving."[14]

"In anticipation of a punitive detachment, the village armed itself with such weapons as it had on hand: some guns, but mainly pitchforks and clubs," wrote Pipes. "Villages nearby joined. The rebels emerged victorious from ensuing encounters with the Red Army. Encouraged by their success, the peasants marched on Tambov, their mass swelling as they neared the provincial capital."[15]

If the Kronstadt rebellion was caused by a lack of freedom and a sense that the revolution had been betrayed, in Tambov, the rebels had a more straightforward motive: they were hungry.

"The Bolsheviks brought in reinforcements, and in September

counterattacked, burning rebellious villages and executing captured partisans," writes Pipes.[16]

While that strategy worked in Georgia and elsewhere, it didn't work in Tambov. The Tambov rebels had a charismatic and brilliant leader, Alexander Antonov. Antonov was a member of the Socialist Revolutionary Party, which had been enormously popular among the peasantry before 1918. Indeed, the Socialist Revolutionaries won the 1917 elections to the Constituent Assembly and would have formed the Russian government had the Bolsheviks not forcibly dispersed that Assembly at its first meeting in early 1918.

Antonov's career paralleled that of Stalin in some ways. Both men were involved in "expropriations" (essentially, robberies) in the years following the 1905 revolution, raising money for their parties. Both spent many years in Siberia afterward, returning to Western Russia only in 1917. Antonov took the side of the Left Socialist Revolutionaries when the party split, thus finding himself (for a time) in alliance with the Bolsheviks. Once that alliance collapsed, Antonov returned to his previous role as a terrorist, targeting Bolshevik leaders instead of tsarist ones. Like Kakutsa in Georgia, he had amassed a small group around him and was seen as a folk hero by many.

When Antonov arrived on the scene in September 1920, the rebellious peasants were on the brink of defeat. He organized partisan detachments, which carried out raids on collective farms and railway lines. They sometimes wore Red Army uniforms. After each operation, Antonov's men would return home, melting away into the peasant mass. The Communists struggled to suppress the rebellion. By the end of the year, Antonov had 8,000 men under arms. Most of them were mounted and able to stage cavalry raids. He grew his rebel army to 20,000 and then 50,000 troops using conscription. They engaged in classical partisan warfare, avoiding confrontations with the Red Army. Antonov was ambitious. He called on the Russian people to join him in a march on Moscow.

Meanwhile, the Soviet leaders persisted in calling the rebels "bandits," as they would later do with the Georgians. But they knew better. They understood that the cause of the rebellion was the requisition teams sent out to confiscate grain from the peasants.

It was not until late February 1921—just as the Red Army was invading Georgia—that Antonov-Ovseenko was sent to Tambov to suppress the revolt. He struggled at first but later took extreme measures, including setting up concentration camps, executing hostages, and deporting thousands. Similar tactics would later be used in the suppression of the 1924 uprising in Georgia. Ultimately, the Communists prevailed, and the Tambov revolt was suppressed.

There were some similarities between the three rebellions in Kronstadt, Tambov, and Georgia. They all occurred after the Civil War ended when Soviet power had been established across nearly all of the former tsarist empire.

In all three cases, these were rebellions of workers and peasants led by leftists of various sorts, including anarchists, Socialist Revolutionaries, and Social Democrats. They were not led by monarchists, nobles, priests, kulaks, or capitalists, as the Communists later claimed. And in none of the three rebellions did foreign intervention occur, leaving the rebels in Kronstadt, Tambov, and Georgia alone to fight the Red Army.

The Tambov rebellion was vast and terrifying to the Soviet leaders; Kronstadt was even worse, as it was a naval mutiny at a fortress next to the Soviet capital of Petrograd—and the mutineers were men who had been central to the Bolshevik seizure of power in 1917.

To compare the August 1924 uprising in Georgia to these events now seems rather far-fetched. But Stalin, Zinoviev, and Orjonikidze were convinced in the late summer of 1924 that the Soviet regime was under threat in Georgia. Their panic at what was after all a fairly limited uprising explains what happened next.

CHAPTER 19

Massacre

PAOLO IASHVILI WAS A GEORGIAN WRITER WHO fell victim to the Stalin purges in the 1930s. During the 1924 uprising, his younger brother was executed by the Bolsheviks. Lasha Bakradze tells the story of what happened next:

> Paolo kept this devastating revelation from his mother. He took it upon himself to lead his mother to believe that his brother was alive. For years, he wrote letters on behalf of his dead brother, pretending that he had escaped and was living in Iran. You could see him miserable, forging his dead brother's hand writing.[1]

In her biography of Beria, Amy Knight tells this story:

> Tsitsna Cholokashvili, the young daughter of an opposition leader, found herself moving in and out of Cheka prisons, together with her mother and younger sister, for several years. They endured beatings, starvation, and interrogations at the hands of the Chekists. Cholokashvili described one incident at the Telavi prison during 1924, when a young Chekist was suddenly confronted with his father, who was sentenced to be executed along with a whole group in one night. When ordered to shoot his own father, the young man shot his two superiors. This led to an all-night "blood orgy" in which hundreds of prisoners were massacred. "The streets were red with blood," recalled Cholokashvili.[2]

The story of the murderous Bolshevik response to the Georgian uprising of 1924 is, above all, a human tragedy.

Though the number of insurgents was relatively small, and the whole rebellion lasted barely a week, the Soviet leadership responded energetically and ruthlessly when it was over. News of the massacres spread quickly—including to foreign news services. As early as September 10, *The New York Times* ran a story entitled "24 are executed for Georgia revolt." The source was not the Georgian government-in-exile or any of the opposition groups but the Georgian Communist government itself.

According to the *Times* report:

The death sentence against twenty-four leaders of the uprising in Georgia has been carried into effect, according to an official statement from the Georgian Government. The statement emphasises that amongst those executed were eight of the most important members of the Central Committee of the Social Democratic Party, including General Jugheli, former commander of the Georgian National Army; M. Khomeriki, Chairman of the joint committee of the Anti-Bolshevist parties; M. Tsheyidze, Chairman of the committee of Batum groups.[3]

There was no mention of the fact that men like Jugheli and Khomeriki were in captivity *before* the outbreak of the rebellion and did not participate in it. They were defenseless hostages, brutally murdered by the Cheka. Khomeriki was murdered in a building used by the Cheka in the old part of Tbilisi. Just a few years earlier, he had worked in the same building himself when it housed the Ministry of Agriculture.

The Times also reported that the Communist government had issued an appeal promising "a pardon and a guarantee of personal freedom to those who break with the Social Democrats and declare their willingness to serve the people on the basis of the Soviet regime."[4]

As Donald Rayfield wrote:

At least 980 men, the cream of Georgia's intelligentsia and nobility (95% were from the gentry), were shot on or around 1 September 1924, sentenced by a troika of party officials and Chekists, and executed by Tatars or Azeris. (Many victims were innocent friends or relatives of rebels.) Hundreds of others, including the writer Konstantine Gamsakhurdia, who had returned from internment and diplomatic service in Germany, were sent to Arctic prison camps. Among the few conspirators spared, after frantic lobbying, was the prose writer Mikeil Javakhishvili.[5]

Indeed when workers, years later, came to create Vake Park, where many of the killings took place, they ran across many skeletons buried in pits.[6]

Eyewitness testimony recorded decades later in the United States gives a flavor of the violence unleashed by the Communist regime in the days following the August uprising. Archil Kekelia testified that "in our small village alone, the Communists shot 18 persons in the first week after the insurrection. Among them was a girl of 15 and 2 boys of 16 and 17."[7]

Alexandr Tsomaia's testimony deserves to be quoted at length:

Immediately after the insurrection was put down the Communists started persecuting everybody, regardless of whether they took part, actual active part in the insurrection or not. But of course, it is impossible to state the exact number, but there must have been from 7,000 to 10,000 men and women executed in the first 3 days after the insurrection was put down, and at least 20,000 were sent away to Siberia.

I would like to add just one small note. I have here a list to show the inhumanity with which Communists treated the Georgian nation. I would like to show a list which was published officially by the Communists—they didn't hide it—in the Georgian press at the time and which describes the punishment meted to one of the Georgian villages in which families bearing the same name of Paniashvili were annihilated, and that included men, women, and small children.

This is not an isolated case; on the contrary, it is typical of many, and shows to what degree of cruelty the Communists descended. Men and women were taken from hospital beds and shot; young school children, students, priests, men who had no connection with the insurrection whatsoever. Without trials, without any interrogation, without any verdict, thousands of Georgians, disarmed and powerless, were taken out and murdered in cold blood. There is no family in Georgia which escaped, which did not have at least one of its members murdered. In a few days, the best representatives of the Georgian nation were destroyed.

This was the first large-scale massacre in Georgia, but certainly not the last. In later years, the numbers of executed were to be counted in tens of thousands, and those deported in hundreds of thousands.[8]

Benia Chkhikvishvili was a leading figure in the Social Democratic Party and was the former mayor of Tiflis. He joined Zhordania and the others in exile in France. As a recent book about him put it, "Chkhikvishvili actively participated in the political life of the government in exile. He was involved in the intra-party negotiations about fighting against the occupier regime and the restoration of the independence of Georgia for creating a united front."[9]

Following the decision by the government-in-exile to launch an armed uprising, Benia traveled with Jugheli from France back to Georgia. Jugheli spoke for both of them with his diary entry from Saturday, February 9, 1924:

"I want this diary to be happier than us: I want it to be the last for [sic] the foreign land…. Today, I arrived in Marseille…. Almost 3 years ago I was exactly here: I entered France through Marseille and I am leaving France through it. Benia and I arrived together and we are leaving together…. A destiny truly exists! Three years ago, I was in a vague mood…. Now I am calm, encouraged, and hopeful…. Then, there was no perspective. Now I have a clear and invincible belief…."

It is not clear if Chkhikvishvili shared Jugheli's confidence about the prospects for the rebellion. He certainly knew that he was not obligated to take part, as he was not very well. But according to a recent biography, "he felt obliged to return to the country to help it."

His doubts about the rebellion were known by others, including Shalva Amirejibi, a National Democrat, who wrote that "together with Chkhikvishvili, many Mensheviks also did not share the idea of rebellion."

Chkhikvishvili was not able to visit his family, though his youngest son, then four years old, was brought to the conspiratorial apartment to meet his father. Many years later, the son vaguely remembered that "a man with a beard" was cuddling and kissing him, saying "My son, my son…"

Benia Chkhikvishvili was arrested on June 25, 1924, at the apartment of Aleksandre Landia on Dusheti Street. This was weeks before Jugheli's arrest, and two months before the outbreak of the rebellion. He was questioned by the Cheka two weeks later and lied about why he had returned to Georgia. He insisted that he was no longer connected to Zhordania and the Social Democrats. He had come to collect his family and move them all to Czechoslovakia.

The diligent Chekists noted his belongings, which were confiscated: "one thermometer, a piece of chemical pencil, two collars, braces, belt, watch, small dictionary."

From a form he filled in upon his arrest, we learn that Benia had been a member of the Social Democratic Party since 1900 and had held several important posts in the Georgian government before the Soviet invasion. Among other things, he was governor-general of the Tiflis district.

On July 30, Benia was sentenced to five years in strict isolation in a Russian labor camp. Writing with a chemical pencil on a shirt, he sent a secret message to his wife, reassuring her. Together with other political prisoners, he was taken to Suzdal prison. And on August 30, two days into the uprising, Cheka boss Felix Dzerzhinsky sanctioned the murder by shooting of key leaders of the Georgian resistance. These included Noe Khomeriki, Gogita Paghava, Giorgi Tsinamdzghvrishvili, Vaso Nodia … and Benia.

They were taken across the border to Russia and were said to have met their deaths bravely. No one knows where they are buried.

The Bolsheviks had gone too far, and they knew this. On September 2, Stalin sent a message to the Transcaucasian Regional Party Committee:

The Central Committee, demanding decisive action to suppress the uprising, categorically rejects the policy of mass executions of those arrested. The Central Committee demands an immediate suspension of executions on the decisions of the Zakchek (Cheka of Transcaucasia).[10]

But the Central Committee's demand was ignored, and the violence continued for many months afterward. According to Amy Knight, "Reprisals continued, with the threat of Georgian Social Democracy used as an excuse, even if the party no longer existed. During the following years, in 1925–1926, at least 500 Georgian Social Democrats were shot without trial."[11]

As recently discovered documents from the Russian state archives show, Stalin was critical of the bloodbath. As Timothy Blauvelt noted, "Stalin expressed his frustration that the Transcaucasian Cheka had executed members of the Committee for Independence without the sanction of the Central Committee in Moscow, and after they had signed their renunciation. This deprived the regime of the moral high ground both domestically and abroad, especially when it became clear that the insurgents had spared the lives of the party members taken prisoner during the uprising."[12]

The victims were mostly not insurgents, and they were not killed on the battlefield. These were executions of unarmed, defenseless civilians. This was not an act of self-defense by an embattled Soviet regime, but revenge. While the number of those killed was not on the scale of the mass murder that had taken place across Russia during the Civil War, it was catastrophic for Georgia, and thousands of innocent lives were lost. In addition to the thousands killed, tens of thousands were deported to Siberia and Central Asia. A reign of terror was unleashed in Georgia that would be remembered for decades.

It would also have unexpected repercussions on the international Left. More than the rebellion itself, its suppression caused the rift between the Socialist and Communist movements to become permanent.

CHAPTER 20

Winter in Tiflis

THE MASSACRE IN GEORGIA FOLLOWING the defeat of the 1924 uprising led directly to massacres of people seen as being in opposition to the regime— whether or not they participated in the fighting.

As the newly-opened Museum of Repressed Writers in Tbilisi puts it:

> Among those who perished in the mass shootings during the days of the uprising were a group of writers and poets—founders of a secret resistance organisation; they were imprisoned in Metekhi prison by authorities loyal to Moscow on political charges associated with supporting Georgian independence. The end of mass shootings by the regime in answer to Damkom's request, saved the lives of many other imprisoned writers. Some of these writers were freed in the political amnesty of the following November, while others were sent to labour camps.

We know of several poets and writers who were killed by the Soviet regime on the same day—28 August 1924, just as the uprising began in Chiatura.

Among them was Daniel Pipia. Pipia was a poet, folklorist and linguist. He was a Social Democrat and was arrested by the Cheka in March 1922. Two and a half years later, he was shot in Tiflis.

Another poet who fell into the hands of the Cheka was Ambrosi Chelidze. Chelidze was a member of the Young Marxists' Organisation, the youth section of the Georgian Social Democratic Party. He was arrested by the Cheka in December 1923 and waited eight months to be murdered by them.

The third poet was Poka Kekelidze. His pen name was "potoli," meaning leaf. Kekelidze too was a member of the Young Marxists' Organisation, and he was arrested by the Cheka in September 1923. Almost a year after his arrest, the Cheka shot him.

Davit Kartsivadze, also a poet, was a former political prisoner under the tsarist regime and a Social Democrat. He was arrested by the Cheka in May 1922 and shot after three months.

Nikoloz Kvernadze, a Social Democratic writer and playwright, was picked up by the Cheka in January 1924 and shot by them seven months later.[1]

Not all the Georgian writers killed by Cheka were Social Democrats. For example, Giorgi (Gigla) Garsiashvili, a writer and publicist, was a leader of the youth wing of the National Democratic Party. He was arrested for a second time by the Cheka in February 1924 and shot in Tiflis.

Mikheil Bochorishvili is the only writer we know of who was arrested *during* the uprising. A leader of Georgia's small Socialist Revolutionary Party, he was not initially killed and instead received a ten-year sentence. But he did not escape what the Cheka euphemistically called the "supreme measure of punishment." He was shot on September 17, 1937, while in exile in the town of Kolpashevo, Tomsk Oblast.

Nearly all of these writers had been in prison during the time that the uprising was being planned and certainly played no role in it. That did not matter for Beria and his men. They were guilty because they supported the Social Democrats, the National Democrats, and the Socialist Revolutionaries.

As Lasha Bakradze wrote in an article about a group of Georgian writers known as the "Blue Horns":

> The relatively liberal attitude of the Communist rulers in Tbilisi attitude towards artists came to an abrupt end following the failed anti–Soviet uprising in Georgia in 1924. The party now demanded that writers make a firm commitment to Communist ideas and to Party policies. So-called "fellow travellers" were no longer needed. The Blue Horns attempted to put themselves at the service of Socialist construction and to adapt to the growing political pressure.[2]

The effect on Georgian culture was profound. A chill could be felt in the air, as was happening all over the Soviet Union. And things would get worse—much worse—in the following decade.

CHAPTER 21

Beria's Secret Speech

LONG BEFORE IT BEGAN IN AUGUST 1924, Beria and the Cheka knew that the uprising was coming. They told imprisoned leaders of the Social Democrats, including Jugheli, that they knew everything, and that resistance was futile. Jugheli seems to have believed them and called upon the rebels to cancel their plans. There are, however, differing interpretations of what Jugheli meant in his message to his comrades. Some historians believe that instead of calling on them to abandon the insurrection, he was calling on them to go ahead.

We don't know exactly how the Cheka learned about the uprising that began on August 28 in Chiatura. There has been some speculation, and we have the extraordinary "testimony" of Beria himself.

The Soviet secret police, like its tsarist predecessor (the Okhrana), wanted everyone to think that it was all-knowing and all-seeing. The Chekists wanted the leaders of the Soviet government to trust them, rely upon them, and, if necessary, even fear them. And they wanted opponents of the Soviet regime to feel that fear, too. But there is evidence that much of what was going on in Georgia in the run-up to the 1924 insurrection was *not* known to the Chekists.

Opposition activists inside Georgia meticulously planned the insurrection. Zhordania and the government-in-exile, which he led in France, laid out the broad strategic perspective for the revolt. It was through the representatives of the Social Democratic party in Istanbul that most communications with Georgia took place. The Cheka picked some of this up, but not all of it. In the early 1920s, for example, the Cheka did not have good contacts inside the Georgian emigre community in France. That would change later on.

Throughout the 1920s, there was growing mistrust among the Georgian exiles between individuals and political parties. This led, in some cases, to violence. The Cheka encouraged this sort of thing. In that context, we have to understand an extraordinary secret speech given by Beria in 1930, six years after the uprising.

"You are aware of cases when a member of [an] anti–Soviet organization governing body would provide us with information about the other with the goal to remove the rival and take his place," Beria told his audience of Communist Party loyalists.[1]

"We would receive written information notifying us where certain persons worked and what organizations they belonged to," Beria said. "We achieved our goal. As a result, we arrested many influential persons from various parties."

Initially, Beria merely acknowledged that members of one party might have informed on a rival party. But then he became very specific: "We have also many cases when one party, for example, [the] National Democratic Party, would provide information about the members of another party, in order to get rid of them," he said.

Referring to the events of six years earlier, at the time of the 1924 national uprising, he explained: "You remember well that during the national revolt, National Democrats wanted to appear in the leadership of the movement in order to reach political hegemony. That is why they fought against Mensheviks using the above-indicated methods."

Beria offered ever more specific details. "Firstly, we received from them [the National Democrats] information about Tsinamdzgvrishvili, their committee member, who was strictly preaching for joint work with Mensheviks," he recalled. Presumably, the Cheka acted on this intelligence about a National Democrat encouraging unity of action with the Social Democrats, something which they were keen to prevent. We know that the Cheka arrested other moderate National Democrats who supported joint work with the Social Democrats.

According to Beria, the National Democrats also set out to destroy the Social Democrats' military organizations. They gave the Cheka details about Vasil Nodia, a Social Democratic member of the Constituent Assembly, who was killed during the uprising on August 31, 1924.

Beria also named the National Democrats as responsible for the capture of Jugheli himself. "With their help, we managed to detain Jugheli," Beria declared, "and they were the ones to send to us the conspiracy plan by post, through which we managed to have Jugheli admit everything."

Beria spoke about the original plan for the revolt, which focused on capturing the capital, Tiflis. Had the rebels succeeded, Beria said, "we would have found ourselves in a quite difficult situation since all Menshevik armed forces were concentrated there."

The rebels' plan had been to first attack the Cheka headquarters in the city. The post office and armored trains would also be seized. It was a comprehensive plan, and the rebels even had the addresses of the homes of leading Bolsheviks, including Orjonikidze. In some cases, they even had copies of the keys to those homes.

The rebellion was planned from Istanbul, with Jugheli and others in charge, and the Damkom inside the country approved it. The Cheka likely learned of the plan in Istanbul, where they had sources.

According to Beria, the National Democrats wanted to organize the rebellion with a different plan, relying on Kakutsa Cholokashvili, who by this time supported them rather than the Social Democrats. Because of this rivalry between the opposition parties, Beria said, "it was easier for us to put down the revolt."

Beria described the "discord between these two anti–Soviet parties" as rendering an excellent service to the Cheka and noted that "we have been receiving this information from National Democrats."

Is Beria's account plausible? Could the National Democrats have been responsible for leaking the secrets of the uprising to the Soviets?

Despite previous differences, by 1924, the Social Democrats and National Democrats were working together in the Damkom and in exile, planning the insurrection. But there is evidence that the National Democrats continued to detest Zhordania and his party, disliking them almost as much as they disliked the Bolsheviks. The National Democrats had their own underground in 1921, and there were rumors then that some of their generals plotted to capture Social Democratic leaders inside Georgia.

Beria is certainly not a trustworthy source of information. The Cheka had used the tactics of divide and rule in Georgia as elsewhere.

The case of General Giorgi Mazniashvili is significant for that reason. Mazniashvili had commanded Georgian forces during the Soviet invasion in 1921. However, he was not trusted by the Georgian Social Democrats in exile, who believed that he may have cooperated with the Bolsheviks before he left the country. According to one report, Mazniashvili later failed to do something that Orjonikidze had ordered him to do. The Cheka, aware of his "immense authority both in and outside Georgia," decided to discredit him. According to one Georgian historian, "At first he was accused of revealing 1924 uprising plans to the Extraordinary

Commission [Cheka], then involvement in a financial scandal and some kind of love affair."[2]

In other words, the Cheka already had experience with falsely accusing Georgians of being informers, as a way of undermining their credibility. This may also be the case with Beria's speech naming the National Democrats as the source of Cheka intelligence about the 1924 revolt. Maybe in his 1930 speech, Beria once again tried to poison the atmosphere and turn the parties against one another.

In any event, the Social Democrats were well aware of the hostility felt towards them by some National Democrats and the rumors that their rival party had fed information to the Cheka. But they chose not to go public with the news.

Whatever the source of the Cheka's information, the existence of informers is not in doubt. The information they gave to Beria and his colleagues allowed the Soviet regime to prepare in advance, to arrest key leaders like Jugheli, and to ensure the defeat of the insurrection. Without that information, whoever provided it, the rebellion might have turned out entirely differently.

CHAPTER 22

The Treason
of the Intellectuals

JULIEN BENDA'S SHORT 1927 BOOK, *La Trahison des Clercs* (*The Treason of the Intellectuals*), caused a bit of a stir when it was first published. Benda did not write about the Georgian uprising that had taken place just three years earlier. But his book described in great detail the strange phenomenon of what he called "clerks"—intellectuals who were perfectly happy to tell lies in support of powerful authoritarian regimes. Benda's book has remained in print ever since it was first published.

According to Benda, some characteristics of those "clerks" included a "cult of cruelty" as well as a "cult of success." He described the latter as "the teaching which says that when a will is successful that fact alone gives it a moral value, whereas the will which fails is for that reason alone deserving of contempt."[1]

For many European intellectuals in the 1920s, the success of the Bolsheviks—and their shameless cruelty—made them admirable. Their defeated opponents, including the Russian Mensheviks and the Georgian Social Democrats, were dismissed with contempt. For some of those intellectuals, the crushing of the Georgian revolt of 1924 allowed them to demonstrate their loyalty to the successful (and very cruel) Soviet regime.

Clara Zetkin was a legend on the international Left. By 1924, the 67-year-old was known around the world for her work building Socialist women's organizations and for establishing International Women's Day. She had been active in the left wing of the German Social Democratic Party and was a close ally and friend of Rosa Luxemburg. Together with Luxemburg, after the Bolshevik coup d'état in 1917, she broke with the Social Democrats to join the new Communist Party of Germany. Her work took her, for a time, to Moscow, where she was given assignments by the Communist International, including being put in charge of Communist work among women around the world.

Henri Barbusse and Clara Zetkin. Communist celebrities tasked with white-washing the massacres in Georgia in 1924 (author's collection).

Following the brief uprising in Georgia in 1924, the scale of the massacres carried out by the Cheka became known around the world. The Georgian Social Democrats received lists of names of those whom the Cheka executed. They shared those lists widely and appealed for solidarity. For the leadership of the Comintern, this was a public relations nightmare. They needed to quickly publicize an alternative version of what had just happened in Georgia. Zetkin was sent to Tiflis.[2]

Her visit to Georgia forced Zetkin to confront the reality of what had just happened—the large-scale executions of innocent men and women, many of whom had had nothing to do with the uprising.

During Zetkin's visit to Georgia, the wives of the victims of the Red Terror reached out to her and confronted her. When Zetkin insisted that the uprising was carried out by the rich, the nobles, and the church, the widow of one of the rebels, David Dvali, threw his clothes at her, to prove that he was an ordinary working man.

The local Communist leadership in Georgia was keen to play down the scale of the revolt and told Zetkin that only about 320 had died. Researchers today give a much higher number, some arguing that over 12,500 were shot by the Soviets.[3]

Zetkin's report was published in 1926 in a book called *Imbefreiten Kaukasus* (*In the Liberated Caucasus*). It was a complete whitewash of the crimes committed by the Communist rulers of Georgia and their Russian allies.

As the American Trotskyist Max Shachtman wrote in an obituary of Zetkin in 1933, "The peculiar triumph of Stalinism … meant for her, as for all revolutionists who failed to choose the alternative of open struggle, a gag in the mouth, a paralyzing of the will, a terrible spiritual degradation."[4] That spiritual degradation is nowhere more apparent than in Zetkin's reaction to the 1924 uprising in Georgia.

Henri Barbusse was an acclaimed French author in 1924. Even today, he is spoken of with reverence. One recent account summarized his life by noting that "after World War I, Henri Barbusse joined the French Communist Party and continued to write pacifist and socialist pieces. The Nazis blacklisted and burned works by Barbusse—champion of pacifism and radical social reforms—because of his leftist ideology."[5]

Barbusse is remembered as a pacifist, social reformer and Socialist. He was an idealist, and he was naturally drawn to the Esperanto movement, with its vision of a universal language as a path to world peace. He was the honorary president of the first congress of the left-wing Esperantist group known as Sennacieca Asocio Tutmonda (SAT) which was initially sympathetic to Soviet Russia. But Barbusse would not have stayed active for very long in SAT, as the organization under the leadership of the fiery Eugene Lanti eventually became quite critical of the Communist regime. (Lanti, as I mentioned earlier, played a role in turning a young George Orwell into an anti–Stalinist.)

Barbusse's Esperanto-speaking comrades in the Soviet Union eventually became victims of the Stalin Terror as the Communists turned on them. There is no evidence that he spoke out in their defense.

Barbusse lent his name to, and headed up, a wide variety of Communist front organizations supporting peace and social justice. He was a loyal and disciplined member of the French Communist Party, subject to its authority and, like Clara Zetkin, obeying orders from the Comintern in Moscow.

Barbusse was asked by the Soviet regime to use his considerable influence and moral authority to explain away what the Communists were doing in Georgia. He did so in his 1929 book, *Voici ce qu'on a fait de la Géorgie* (*This is what we did with Georgia*).

In 1927, Barbusse met with Stalin on the eve of his visit to Georgia. He was possibly the first European writer to meet the new Soviet leader. Barbusse came to Stalin with a concrete problem. According to Michael David-Fox, he "needed to distinguish Soviet political violence, including the integration of independent Georgia in 1920 [*sic*], from the fascist violence he was mobilizing intellectuals against in Europe."[6]

"How should he explain to Europeans the difference between fascist ('white') and Red Terror?" It was a good question and, perhaps unintentionally went to the very heart of the problem. What was the difference between fascist terror and Communist terror? Stalin fended it off by saying that after 1918, "there was no such thing as Red Terror."[7]

Stalin spun a fairy tale history that Barbusse was all too willing to accept. The shootings during 1918 did not repeat themselves, he reassured the French writer. "If it weren't for the ruthlessness and strength of the capitalists, moreover, the Soviet Union might have been able to abolish the death penalty." Stalin added "Of course the death penalty is an unpleasant thing. Who finds it pleasant to kill people?"

Barbusse replied, telling Stalin "This is absolutely correct. In current conditions eliminating the death penalty would be suicide for Soviet power."[8]

Barbusse wrote his Georgia book as "part travelogue, playing on the exotic locale, part semi-fictional interviews with natives, and part political tract."[9] It countered charges that the Soviets had engaged in a kind of "red imperialism" in their 1921 invasion of Georgia. And it was a dress rehearsal for Barbusse's later hagiographic biography of the Soviet leader in 1935.

Barbusse was concerned that the world was getting its facts wrong about what had happened in Georgia at the time of the August 1924 uprising. Referring to what today would be called "mainstream media," Barbusse said that the "*fausses nouvelles*" they published, if collected in a book, would form an enormous encyclopedia. Decades before the term "fake news" began to be widely used, Barbusse used the same expression to describe how non–Communist writers were "lying" about what happened in Georgia in 1924. His book was intended to set the record straight.

The August uprising, he reported, had been preceded by "uprisings fomented by former officers"—never by workers or peasants—who as their very first act when seizing a village would return the land to the nobles. Barbusse seemed unaware of the fact the Georgian Social Democratic government had given the land to the peasants in a very successful agrarian reform during the period of independence.

He wrote that the Georgian rebels were keen to get foreign support, especially from France. He claimed that they negotiated directly with General Maxime Weygand, one of the most important French commanders. Weygand had already helped fight the Bolsheviks in Poland. Barbusse claimed that the Georgian government-in-exile had also requested financial support from the government led by Aristide Briand, a former Socialist. He did not mention whether Weygand or Briand turned out to be helpful for the Georgians, though he was undoubtedly aware that no foreign forces came to Georgia's assistance in 1924.

Barbusse believed that the anti–Soviet Georgians used the crushing of the 1924 uprising for their own propaganda purposes and that, for them, it was even more important than the Red Army invasion in 1921, which may well have been true. He was furious at what he thought were exaggerations about the number of those killed.

"Villages destroyed by artillery; mass imprisonments, executions … tortures, refinements of cruelty comparable to those employed by the police and governments of fascism and white terror"—these were lies spread by anti–Soviet forces, he wrote. They did not reflect the reality, as Barbusse saw it, of a small rebellion easily crushed with very few casualties. He was stung by the comparisons being made between the behavior of the Communists and those of the fascists in Italy.

Barbusse traveled around Georgia and concluded that all talk of killings and atrocities was wildly exaggerated by opponents of the regime. "For example, with regard to the villages destroyed by the artillery.... I was able to go and see them, and to see that the artillery had never been used," he wrote. Remember that this visit took place several years after the 1924 rebellion.

He dismissed reports that it had become "impossible to move about without risking aggression, imprisonment and death.... I spoke to many people who had gone to Georgia immediately after the uprising and who all categorically denied this." Barbusse learned from his Georgian friends that "at that time it was safe and free to move around in any part of Georgia."

He denied that some of the Social Democrats who were captured were victims of torture by the Cheka. "I never received any accusations of ill-treatment," he wrote. As for executions of prominent Social Democrats, many of whom were already in Cheka prisons before the uprising and who took no part in it, Barbusse insisted that they should not be called "hostages"—which, of course, is precisely what they were.

"These prisoners were all murderers and executioners with countless crimes on their record," he wrote. And it was not just what they did in 1924, supposedly colluding with foreign imperialists, priests, and tsarist officers against the new Soviet regime. It was even what they did during the years of Georgian independence that justified their murders. The former head of the People's Guard, Jugheli, was a "monster," he wrote.

In his 1953 book, *The Georgian Question Before the Free World*, Constantin Kandelaki wrote this about Barbusse: "The famous French novelist put his talent as a writer and his literary fame at the service of Bolshevik propaganda: to justify what the Soviets had done in Georgia. He wrote a whole book on Georgia in which he reproduced blindly everything told to him by Russian and Georgian Communists."[10]

According to Kandelaki, Barbusse's 1927 book did not go unanswered. A Georgian émigré named David Sharashidze wrote a book called *Barbusse, les Soviets et la Géorgie* [*Barbusse, the Soviets and Georgia*] which was published in 1929. Karl Kautsky, still doing what he could to support the Georgian Social Democrats nearly a decade after he visited the country, wrote the preface to Sharashidze's book.

"Barbusse's book not only gave them an opportunity to refute step by step his story, full of untrue and falsified statements, but also of presenting once again to foreign readers some true pages from Georgian history."

Sharashidze, wrote Kandelaki, "accomplished his task with talent."[11]

In his preface, Kautsky praised Sharashidze, writing that he not only demolished Barbusse but "what is more important, he reveals the situation of Georgia under the scourge of the Kremlin.... Thus, once again, the Bolshevist attempt to counteract the sympathy aroused in the free world by the Georgian question, had turned against the Bolshevists themselves."[12]

Kandelaki was certain that the books by Zetkin and Barbusse were completely ineffectual as propaganda. "Bolshevist propaganda concerning Georgia," he wrote, "never had any effect on well-informed people; in every country, it remained isolated in the Communist press and their editions did not go beyond the circles of Communist militants or sympathisers."[13]

That may have been true in much of the outside world, but inside Georgia, it was another story entirely. The Soviet myths about the 1924 uprising were taught to generations of schoolchildren and written up in the history books. It would not be until Georgia regained its independence in 1991 that the Georgian people could begin to learn the true history of their country.

Even if Barbusse and Zetkin persuaded very few people outside of the Soviet Union with their books, the poisonous lies being told about Georgia were not limited to Communist propaganda. As we shall see in the next chapter, even Social Democrats who should have known better failed to show solidarity with their Georgian comrades, and on some occasions lied as brazenly as Barbusse and Zetkin had.

CHAPTER 23

Where Were Georgia's Allies?

WHEN CLARA ZETKIN WROTE HER DEFENSE of the Soviet response to the uprising, she at least had the excuse of having left the Social Democratic Party and become a Communist. She and Henri Barbusse were bound by Party discipline to repeat the official line, even if they knew it was not true.

But as we shall see, some Social Democratic and Labor leaders who withdrew their support for the Georgians or downplayed the scale of what had just happened in Georgia had no such excuse.

The Georgians who rose up in August 1924 anticipated that their rebellion would have support within the country, among some of Georgia's neighbors, and in the wider world. There were hopes that Britain and France might send help to the rebels. But in the end, the Georgians stood alone against Soviet Russia.

While their neighbors in the region and the European powers might not provide help, the Georgians were confident that they would at the very least receive the support of the international Socialist movement. This meant above all the support of the British Labour Party and the French Socialists, whose leaders had been part of the 1920 delegation to the country.

This hope, which was shared both by the government-in-exile near Paris and the Georgians inside the country, fit perfectly with the Soviet propaganda of that time and afterward.

According to the Soviet regime, the insurrection of 1924 was a foreign plot, hatched in connivance with British and French imperialism, backed by the leaders of the Second International—including Ramsay MacDonald, the newly elected British Prime Minister and head of the country's first Labour government.

This interpretation was the one taught in schools and published in books and newspapers in the Soviet Union (including Soviet Georgia) for nearly seventy years after the uprising. And while it had indeed been the hope of the Georgian rebels that they would enjoy some support from the

European powers, or at the very least the solidarity of the Social Democratic and Labor parties, this did not turn out to always be the case.

Western governments did not come to Georgia's aid. Even the minimal support displayed by French warships in 1921, when Georgia was first invaded by the Soviets, was not available this time. The newly formed League of Nations proved to be useless.

Maybe the Georgians should not have been surprised. The Soviets had won the fight in 1921; Georgia would not win back its independence any time soon, and there was, therefore, little point in protesting. Furthermore, lucrative trade deals with the new Soviet Russian regime were due to be signed, commerce would resume, and money was to be made.

Britain's betrayal of Georgia began early—in 1921—long before the election of a Labour government when MacDonald and his party were seen as pro–Georgian following their visit the previous year. In March of that year, as David Lang wrote, the

> British and Soviet governments signed a trade agreement in which [Prime Minister] Lloyd George undertook inter alia to refrain from anti–Soviet activity in all territories which had formed part of the old Tsarist empire. This effectively precluded any British intervention against the Bolsheviks in Georgia, which Great Britain had recognized as an independent sovereign state less than two months previously. Small wonder that the defeated Georgian patriots were loud in their denunciation of perfidious Albion.[1]

Lang concluded that by 1924, "not one of the great powers which had accorded the Georgian Republic full recognition only three years previously raised a finger to help the Georgian people in their struggle."[2]

When the revolt broke out in August 1924, when it was unclear if the Georgians stood a chance against the Soviets, much sympathy was expressed—in words. The Labour government in Britain was quick to raise the Georgian question at the League of Nations. But once Soviet rule had been re-established, they changed course.

Labour then came under attack in the House of Commons for downplaying the scale of the killings taking place in Tiflis. In a debate in Parliament on October 2, 1924, barely a month after the Georgian insurrection, a Conservative member, Lord Apsley (Allen Bathurst), rose to ask the Prime Minister "whether the occupation of Georgia by the Union of Soviet [Socialist] Republics is recognised by His Majesty's Government or the League of Nations; and whether the right to occupy this country was acquired by treaty or as a mandate from the League of Nations?"[3]

The question was, of course, rhetorical. Apsley was well aware that the Soviet government occupied Georgia as a result of its illegal invasion of the country in 1921 and had no League of Nations mandate to be there.

The Government's response came from Labour MP Arthur Ponsonby, Under Secretary of State for Foreign Affairs, who cited a statement made on behalf of the government some eight months earlier. The British government, he said, "recognise the authority of the Government of the Union of Soviet Socialist Republics as extending to Georgia."[4]

At length, he also explained that "I naturally cannot speak for the League of Nations, nor do His Majesty's Government feel entitled to pronounce on the derivation of that authority, but the Government of the Union certainly hold no mandate from the League." Translated into plain English, Ponsonby was saying that no, the Soviets did not have a mandate from the League of Nations to occupy Georgia. Still, the British government did not "feel entitled" to suggest by what legal authority the Soviets now ruled Georgia.

Not satisfied with this reply, another Conservative MP, Lieut.-Colonel Charles Howard-Bury, began by asking, "Is the Under-Secretary aware that no fewer than 9,000 Georgians have already been executed?"—but was interrupted with cries of "How do you know?," presumably from Labour members.

Howard-Bury was immediately challenged by a Labour MP, John Edmund Mills, who served as Parliamentary Private Secretary to Josiah Wedgwood, then a Labour politician (and descendant of the famous potter). Mills turned to Howard-Bury, saying:

> Before the Under-Secretary replies, may I ask him if his attention has been called to a statement by the Italian Consul at Tiflis to the effect that the reported outbreak was put down by the local people without the aid of troops, that order has been restored since 1st September, that there have been no massacres, and that the 9,000 is merely imagination?[5]

And there, the debate ended.

In just a month, the Labour government had gone from expressing outrage at the Soviet Russian aggression in Georgia, raising the question in the League of Nations, and declaring its shock at the massacres of thousands of Georgians to "correcting" opposition members of Parliament who seemed to be exaggerating the number of those killed. "There had been no massacres" had become Labour's official position on Georgia.

The French Socialists were equally quick to forget their solidarity with the Georgians. Their decision to do so was enabled by the exiled Russian Mensheviks, who were divided in their views on the struggle against the Soviet regime. The Socialists had initially been among those to show the strongest support for independent Georgia, and their leaders Pierre Renaudel, Adrien Marquet, and Alfred Inghels traveled as part of the international Socialist delegation to Georgia in 1920. In 1921, the French Socialists had called upon "the French workers to protest against the occupation of the Georgian Socialist Democratic Republic by the Bolshevik government of Russia."[6]

But by 1924, much had changed. According to André Liebich, "During the Georgian insurrection in 1924, the [Russian] Mensheviks were asked whether French socialist deputies should take a firm position and risk bringing down the Herriot government. They counseled moderation, thus allowing their French comrades to remain inactive in good conscience."[7]

Even if the Russian Mensheviks could not bring themselves to side with their former comrades in Georgia, the idea that they would advise the French Socialists to avoid taking a "firm position" against the Russians seems rather unkind, to say the least.

But the Georgians did win a victory of sorts in France less than two months after the uprising. According to Timothy Blauvelt, "On 28 October 1924 France gave *de jure* recognition to the USSR, but 'only to those territories where Soviet power is recognized by the population,' which the GiE [Georgian Government-in-Exile] viewed as a victory, especially as this provision allowed for the GiE to preserve its position in France with its diplomatic privileges as the recognized representation of independent Georgia."[8]

The actions of the British Labour Government were rooted in the desire to put the Georgian uprising behind them and to move on towards normalizing relations—especially trade—with Soviet Russia. But their betrayal of the Georgians was overshadowed by the actions of leaders of Britain's trade unions just a few months later.

CHAPTER 24

The British
Trade Union Delegation

On December 6, 1924, some three months after the Georgian uprising was crushed, this headline appeared in the *Daily Herald*: "TUC Delegates Satisfied by Inquiry on Spot." The *Daily Herald*, published in London, was the official newspaper of the British Trades Union Congress (TUC). The headline referred to a group of senior trade unionists who were visiting Soviet Georgia. The trade unionists were "studying life in the Georgian Republic in all its details and from all sides." That was somewhat of an exaggeration, as at least one side—the Georgian labor movement—was completely ignored.

The *Daily Herald* reported that the TUC delegates "had a prolonged conversation with several former members of the Menshevik Party." The Georgian Social Democratic Party had been forced to dissolve itself the previous year. Some of the Social Democrats had then gone over to the Communist side, with more joining them after the crushing of the August uprising. By "former members" of the Social Democratic Party, the *Daily Herald* meant people who had been coerced into becoming supporters of the Communist regime.

One member of the British delegation was TUC Vice President A.A. Purcell. Purcell had participated in the founding meeting of the Communist Party of Great Britain a few years earlier and was now advocating the affiliation of the Communists to the Labour Party—which the Labour majority opposed. He was definitely on the more pro–Soviet side of the British labor movement.

Following his 1924 visit to Georgia, Purcell was quoted as saying: "I have been in the midst of the Georgian workers. I am convinced of their economic success and of the falseness of the information regarding Georgia circulated in Europe."

That "false information" was being circulated primarily by supporters of the Georgian government-in-exile, who were Social Democrats.

Fred Bramley, the secretary of the General Council of the Trades Union Congress, said that "Soviet Georgia is alive because it is supported by the people."

Ben Tillett of the Transport Workers' Union said: "The Soviet [Union] and Trans-Caucasia are living together peacefully. The self-determination of a nation has been realised here in such a degree as Europe can only dream of."[1]

Purcell, Bramley, and Tillett were known Communist sympathizers who regularly met with Soviet officials. In Georgia, they and the other TUC delegates were asked to pose and be photographed—intentionally—in the same places where Ramsay MacDonald and other Socialist leaders had stood during their visit four years earlier.

The report of the TUC delegates attracted furious denunciations by labor movement leaders in other countries. One of those was Friedrich Adler, the Austrian Social Democrat who convened the 1922 Berlin meeting of the three Internationals. By 1924, partly as a result of the failure of that meeting, Adler and his supporters had reunited with the Second International.

In a booklet published as *The Anglo-Russian Report: a criticism of the report of the British trades union delegation to Russia, from the point of view of international socialism*, Adler made a devastatingly effective attack on the pro–Bolshevik report of the British trade unionists. He found unedited Soviet propaganda throughout the TUC report.

For example, the delegates wrote about the "enthusiastic demonstration of workers and Trade Union officials" with which the Delegation was received in Tiflis. According to the British trade unionists, "This demonstration appeared to reflect the strong, united approval of the workers in the present system of government in Georgia."[2]

Adler wrote:

What the Delegation itself relates in the Preface is in the main a harmless description of its itinerary and stopping stations. Occasionally the political bias breaks out somewhat naively, as in the conversation with the railway conductors ... who "discussed freely the conditions under which they lived and stated frankly their personal objections with regard to some of the restrictions under which they worked," from which the conclusion is drawn that "this to some extent refutes the idea that expressions of this kind were unsafe or unwise in Soviet Russia."[3]

Though Socialists like Adler were disappointed with the behavior and report of the TUC delegate, the Soviets were delighted. Fifty years after the delegation's visit, you can still feel how pleased the Communists were with their propaganda success. As late as the 1970s, the Soviet historian Trifonov wrote that "a delegation from the English trade unions that visited Transcaucasia in the fall of 1924 published a forthright refutation of the malicious inventions of the capitalist and reformist press on the situation in Georgia."[4]

But in 1924, the Georgian trade unionists were furious. They had welcomed the British TUC delegates with a memorandum that began:

> Comrades, The workers of Georgia welcome with joy the news of your arrival: they are sure you will acquaint yourselves with the state of thought in Georgia, objectively and impartially, which qualities of investigation characterise best every conscious and true leader of the workers. By acquainting yourselves impartially with what has happened in Georgia during the recent years, you will do a priceless service to our martyred country, whose working class have always served self-sacrificingly Justice and Freedom. Full of this hope, we welcome you and appeal to you to acquaint yourselves with our country and to study the regime under which the Georgian working-class labours to-day.

But in a pamphlet published the following year, the tone had completely changed:

> When the British Trade-Union Delegation under the leadership of Purcell was in Georgia last December, the old, now illegal, Executive of the Georgian trade-unions transmitted to the delegates a memorandum giving a short account of the suffering of the Georgian workers and of the whole nation under the occupation regime. The Memorandum finishes proposing: "If you wish, in view of the above, to meet us, we shall arrange this with pleasure and verbally communicate to you many facts which will throw light on the Occupation regime." But the Delegation did not pay attention either to the Memorandum or the proposal of our comrades. The delegates did not even wish to see the senders of the Memorandum or to ask them for information concerning the facts mentioned in the Memorandum. They simply put a number of questions to the Soviet Authorities about their action in Georgia, and on the basis of that one-sided information wrote their report which consists of nothing but praise for the Occupation regime in our country.[5]

They then proceeded to describe the ruthless persecution of the Georgian trade unions following the Soviet invasion in 1921.

In addition, the Georgian trade unionists took their British comrades to task for claiming that Bolshevik rule had led to big increases in exports. They insisted that genuine statistics from 1920 show "that trade was growing whilst under the [Soviet] occupation it remained stationary." The British delegates also reported that the number of industrial workers had doubled under the Communist regime. The Georgians pointed out that even the official statistics did not bear this out. As the Georgian trade unionists explained, "This is the result of the fact that the Bolsheviks have two sets of statistics, one for their own use and the other for foreigners." The British delegates were delighted with the near absence of reported unemployment—but the Georgians pointed out that under the Social Democrats when Georgia was an independent country "the number of unemployed never exceeded a few hundred" and added: "The Delegation might have obtained information on this subject if they had consulted our Illegal Trade Union Bureau."

The British TUC delegates also accepted the official Soviet line regarding the number of those killed following the 1924 uprising. According to the British report, "there were 3,000 victims" which is ten times the number Clara Zetkin admitted to. Despite being more accurate in describing the scale of the killing carried out by the Cheka, those who died were described "as if they had fallen in partisan fights" rather than being executed by the Bolsheviks following the defeat of the rebellion. As the Georgians wrote, summing up the British report:

> In other words the Bolsheviks have not shot political prisoners or peaceful citizens, but on the contrary, according to the Delegation report, the Mensheviks shot 18 Bolshevik hostages.

The story of the Social Democrats shooting hostages was a complete fabrication. As the Georgian trade unionists wrote, "The Bolsheviks themselves have never accused the rebels of having shot hostages. In fact, the Bolsheviks have reported in their papers that the Mensheviks had not shot any Bolshevik prisoners though they themselves shot Mensheviks by the hundred[s]."

The British Trade Union delegates in their report were lying about what had happened in 1924 even more brazenly than the Bolsheviks themselves.

To prove their case, the Georgian trade unionists produced a photograph of a list of political prisoners who were shot. The list had been published by the Bolsheviks themselves. Those prisoners "had been under arrest long before the rising" and in some cases were shot in Russia, where they were being held. The hostages shot by the Cheka included trade union leaders:

Among those executed were many men well known in the trade-union movement and members of central organisations as for instance, the transport worker V. Nodia, a member of the General Council of the Georgian Trade-Unions, and V. Tsenteradze, a member of the Executive of the General Council and Vice-President of the Central Committee of the railwaymen, and many others.

Some of the statements made by the British trade unionists were not just wrong, but absurd. For example, they claimed that the famous 26 Baku commissars were shot by Georgian Social Democrats in September 1918. As the Georgians wrote, "Even the Bolsheviks never brought such an accusation against the Georgians; they always accused the British who helped the Russian Whites in their struggle against the Bolsheviks in Trans-Caspia."

The Georgian trade unionists concluded their message by saying, "The Report is full of inaccuracies and therefore, if the General Council [of the TUC] is willing to examine in detail the Report and verify how much it differs with the reality we propose it should appoint a special commission to which we could present irrefutable data on the actual condition of Georgia."

No special commission was appointed, and the Georgian trade unionists were ignored.

While the TUC delegation to Georgia and its report mark a significant betrayal, the denunciation of their report by Adler revealed that there were still many in the Social Democratic parties and labor movement who were shocked and angry at the behavior of the Bolsheviks in Georgia.

That anger would lead to a rethinking of the relationship between the Socialist and Communist movements—a rethinking that would result in a final break.

PART III

Socialism and Communism

CHAPTER 25

Red Fascism

OTTO RÜHLE WAS ONE OF THE FOUNDERS of the German Communist Party and one of the first to break ranks over the question of Russia. As early as 1924, while the Georgian Social Democrats were preparing their national insurrection, Rühle explained why no Marxist should support the new Soviet regime in Russia.

"When the socialists in the Russian government, after the victory over tsarism, imagined that a phase of historical development could be skipped and socialism structurally realised, they had forgotten the ABC of Marxist knowledge," he wrote.

In a succinct restatement of the Menshevik viewpoint, which the Georgian Social Democrats shared, Rühle wrote that Socialism "can only be the outcome of an organic development which has capitalism developed to the limits of its maturity."[1]

After splitting from the Communists, Rühle wrote many books and articles, including a biography of Karl Marx. By 1939, his analysis of Soviet Russia had developed. He no longer wrote of it as socialism gone wrong or a premature attempt by genuine Socialists to skip stages of history. His earlier ideas about it being a "bourgeois revolution" were set aside. Instead, he saw the Stalinist system that had emerged from the Bolshevik revolution as a new form of class society, which he called "totalitarian."

"Russia must be placed first among the new totalitarian states," he wrote at a time when totalitarian states were growing stronger by the day and were about to embroil the world in a new war. Soviet Russia, he wrote, "was the first to adopt the new state principle. It went furthest in its application. It was the first to establish a constitutional dictatorship, together with the political and administrative terror system which goes with it. Adopting all the features of the total state, it thus became the model for those other countries which were forced to do away with the democratic state system and to change to dictatorial rule." He concluded his description of Soviet society with this extraordinary sentence: "Russia was the example for fascism."[2]

In branding Soviet Russia as an example of fascism, indeed as the model for a fascist state, he was not exaggerating for effect or merely trying to insult his Communist opponents. He genuinely thought that the new regime in Moscow was fascist, like Italy and Germany.

"Whether party 'communists' like it or not, the fact remains that the state order and rule in Russia are indistinguishable from those in Italy and Germany," he concluded. "Essentially, they are alike. One may speak of a red, black, or brown 'soviet state,' as well as of red, black or brown fascism."[3]

Rühle was not the first to conclude that the regime led by Stalin was more similar to Italy and Germany than to any kind of socialism. Among the first to draw that conclusion were some anarchist writers—and the Georgian Social Democrats.

For example, the Italian anarchist Luigi Fabbri described the Russian Communists as "red fascists" as early as 1922, the year that Mussolini came to power in Italy. Red fascists, he wrote, "is the name that has recently been given to those Bolshevik communists who are most inclined to espouse fascism's methods for use against their adversaries."[4]

Fabbri wrote this 17 years before Rühle published his book. The noted Russian anarchist Vsevolod Mikhailovich Eikhenbaum, known by his pseudonym Volin, wrote in 1934 that he had been reading a letter from a fellow anarchist, Alfonso Petrini. Petrini had been banished somewhere inside the Soviet Union. Volin quoted lines from Petrini's message: "They're locking us all up, one by one. Real revolutionaries may not enjoy freedom in Russia. Freedom of the press and freedom of speech have been wiped out, so *there is no difference between Stalin and Mussolini.*"

Voline added that he had emphasized that last phrase because "it is spot on." He added that "for the accuracy of this short phrase and all its ghastly realism to be appreciated, it is essential that we have a deep and clear-cut grasp of fascism: deeper and clearer cut than is generally the case in leftist circles." Voline was convinced that Petrini's declaration was "not as some sort of a catchphrase but as the precise expression of a very sad fact."[5]

Very early on, long before Otto Rühle compared the Stalinist and fascist regimes, the Georgian Social Democrats were also among the very first to note the similarities. In a resolution passed by a "secret conference" of the outlawed Social Democratic Party in Georgia in 1925, a year after the uprising and the massacres, the similarities between the Communists and fascists were noted.

"The persecution of our Party continues with the same vigour," they wrote, noting the torture tactics employed in the "dark and deep dungeons" of the Cheka. The Georgian Social Democrats described these as "*fascist methods* against the members of our Party, shooting them from behind."[6]

In a "Letter to the Working Classes of Germany," the Georgian Social Democrats accused the Soviets of going further than the fascists in their attacks on political opponents: "In spite of the fact that the enemy employ all possible means, even such as would have been never

Otto Rühle, German Communist who broke ranks and later popularized the term "red fascism" to describe the Soviet regime (author's collection).

employed by a Fascist or Tsarist Government, they have failed to break the spirit of our Party, the resistance of our people, and to compel us to leave the battlefield."[7]

Their statement ends with a series of slogans, among them, "*Down with Red Fascism!*"

The Georgian Social Democrats were almost certainly among the first Socialists to use the term "red fascism" to describe the Soviet regime. Their view that the Communist and fascist regimes had much in common would eventually become commonplace, particularly during the Cold War. But in the 1920s, it was unusual.

It was significant not only because of the emotional power of the phrase "red fascism" but also because, in many ways, it was the most accurate description of the new Soviet regime. The Georgian Social Democrats understood precisely what they were dealing with in the new Soviet regime. They understood this because of their experiences in the "dark and deep dungeons" of the Cheka. And what they discovered was that this new society was a form of fascism.

This powerful idea is central to the reasons for the final break between Socialists and Communists. And it took the suppression of the Georgian uprising of 1924 to bring this idea to the fore.

CHAPTER 26

The Birth of
Democratic Socialism

In 1923, the Second International and the so-called "Two and a Half International" (also known as the "Vienna International") merged to create the Labour and Socialist International (LSI). It represented most of the world's Socialist and labor parties. The decision to merge followed the failure of the two Socialist groups to find common ground with the Communist International after the Berlin Conference of 1922. As we have seen, the collapse of those talks was partly due to the disagreement about Georgia.

In September 1924, following the brutal suppression of the uprising in Georgia, LSI's Executive Committee discussed the International's attitude toward Bolshevism and the Soviet regime. A commission was set up to draft a resolution but needed help to come up with something useful. And at this point, a strange thing happened.

Karl Kautsky happened to be at the LSI Executive meeting in September 1924 as a stand-in for the Austrian Social Democrat Otto Bauer. Kautsky and Bauer disagreed strongly on the Russian question. As far back as November 1917, Kautsky was more critical of the Bolsheviks than his younger colleague Bauer.

At this time, Kautsky was no longer the "Pope of Marxism." His waning influence was evident to all. He had spent years in the political wilderness following his decision to quit the German Social Democratic Party and join the breakaway anti-war Independent Social Democratic Party of Germany (USPD). Kautsky no longer edited *Die Neue Zeit*, a journal that had created the Marxist worldview more than any other.

He developed views on the Bolsheviks that were far ahead of their time. His first criticisms of Lenin and his comrades were written just days after the Bolshevik seizure of power. His first full-length book attacking the new Soviet regime, *The Dictatorship of the Proletariat*, appeared in print before the Bolsheviks celebrated their first year as rulers of Russia.

Kautsky's powerful attacks on the Bolsheviks prompted their leaders, Lenin, Trotsky, and Radek, to write book-length responses. To the Bolsheviks, Kautsky was not a weak old opponent. To them, he was still formidable and deserving of attention, if not respect.

At the LSI Executive Committee, Kautsky volunteered to draft a resolution expressing the International's views on Bolshevism. In addition to writing the resolution, Kautsky "also wrote an extensive memorandum in support of his resolution, since he would probably not be present at the next meeting and would therefore be unable to defend his resolution."[1]

As W.H. Roobol wrote, "Although it later became clear that the Russian Mensheviks were in complete disagreement with the content of this resolution, Kautsky was at the time under the impression that he had found the right formula for expressing the views of both the Russian and the Georgian Mensheviks. He was misled by the Russian delegation's moderately positive reactions at the above-mentioned Executive Committee meeting. Eventually, Kautsky's memorandum was published in an altered form."[2]

The victory of the Bolsheviks and the crushing of the Mensheviks inside Russia had led to divisions within the Menshevik Party. Some advocated finding ways to accommodate to life under Communist rule, including giving support to the Soviet regime during the civil war. Others were more hostile to Lenin and his party. The Georgians generally sided with the more militantly anti–Communist wing of the Menshevik movement.

Kautsky's resolution and the short book he wrote to explain it marked a sea change on the international Left. Critics of the Soviets increasingly began speaking of the new Moscow regime as fundamentally no different from fascism.

As Roobol wrote, Kautsky "rejected Bolshevism absolutely and compared it to tsarism. The fight against Bolshevism he treated in the same way as the fight against Mussolini's fascism."[3]

The relationship between the Socialist and Communist movements had changed completely in the two years since they met in room 25 of the Reichstag in Berlin. In the immediate aftermath of the August 1924 uprising in Georgia, the Socialists were now willing to ask the most anti–Communist of them all, Karl Kautsky, to draft a historic resolution—knowing how strongly Kautsky felt. The resolution Kautsky wrote and the short book that explains it in greater detail set the tone for how Socialists would view Soviet Communism for decades to come.

In his 1925 book, *Die Internationale und Sowjetrussland* (*The International and Soviet Russia*), Kautsky summarized his views in the wake of the abortive insurrection in Georgia the previous year. Though his book is a general discussion of Soviet Russia, there are numerous references to Georgia, especially in the conclusion. The 1924 uprising and its bloody suppression were a turning point in Kautsky's thinking, especially regarding how the international Socialist movement should respond to armed rebellions of that type.

Bolshevism, he wrote, "went from being the beneficiary of the revolution to its gravedigger, and today performs only counter-revolutionary functions." The Soviet regime no longer had any positive, revolutionary role to play.[4]

The task of the International, of the Social Democratic parties and the labor movement more broadly, is therefore "to seize every opportunity that may arise to support the Russian people in general and the Russian proletariat in particular in their struggle for liberation."

Thinking no doubt of the recent Georgian uprising, Kautsky wrote, "One must reckon with the possibility that in Russia, the opponents of Bolshevism are preparing armed uprisings against it in order to overthrow it."

Reckoning with the possibility does not mean encouraging it. On the contrary, Kautsky noted that at its first congress, the newly formed Labour and Socialist International "rejected the prepared insurrection as a means of winning democracy in Russia." He believed that this was the correct position and should not be changed.

Drawing on the experience of the Georgian Social Democrats, Kautsky argued that such planned rebellions were "hopeless given [the] balance of power" with the Soviet state. Such rebellions deliver "the best men of the opposition to the Cheka." This was certainly the case in Georgia, where some of the most competent and prominent Social Democrats—the architect of the agrarian reform, Khomeriki, and the leader of the People's Guard, Jugheli, among them—did fall into the hands of the Cheka, which murdered them.

Kautsky added that "no conspiracy remains hidden" from the Cheka, which appeared to be the case regarding Georgia in 1924. The Cheka was not all-knowing as we have seen, but the carefully cultivated image of its omniscience had convinced Kautsky, among many others.

But in addition to what Kautsky called "prepared uprisings," which was undoubtedly the case in Georgia in 1924, there might also be "spontaneous uprisings of the working masses" against the Communist regime. Kautsky felt that such uprisings "can neither be provoked nor hindered at will" and can "achieve great political effects" if extensive enough. Could such uprisings be on the cards in Soviet Russia? Kautsky thought so.

"The conditions in Soviet Russia are so appalling," he wrote, and "the policy of the government so adventurous that we must reckon with the possibility of such uprisings." In those cases, what were Democratic Socialists to do? The next sentence Kautsky wrote may be the most important of his short book, though it appears only on the very last page. It marked a turning point in Socialist thinking about Communism.

"The International," he wrote, "cannot condemn participation in general uprisings of this kind."

"Cannot condemn"—this is not the same as saying "support," but it is probably the first significant document coming from a leading European Socialist indicating just how wide the gap had become between two movements that just a decade earlier had been united in a single International.

Kautsky argued that if the International did condemn such uprisings, it would not be able to prevent them. Furthermore, its condemnation of such revolts "would cause the outraged masses [in Russia] to entrust themselves entirely to the leadership of the reactionaries who, like us, though for very different reasons, are fighting Bolshevism."

This, too, marked a significant shift in Socialist thinking. Acknowledging that there were others who "like us" were fighting against the Soviet regime opened the possibility (which seemed quite distant in 1925) that Socialists may well have allies in the fight. This would become much clearer in the coming years, especially with the outbreak of the Cold War two decades later.

Kautsky was clear that the danger of reactionaries taking advantage of an armed revolt against the Communists may have been a problem in most parts of the Soviet Union but not Georgia. Georgia was the exception.

"Only in Georgia," he wrote, "was there never any danger that an uprising, if it succeeded, could serve reaction. Every uprising there had to be aimed at winning national independence from any Russian regime" and that uprising "had to be directed from the outset as much against tsarism as against Moscow Bolshevism." This was certainly the case with the 1924 uprising in Georgia.

Despite the later claims of Soviet historians that the rebels of 1924 aimed to restore the land-owning nobility, Kautsky explained the reality in Georgia, which he knew first-hand following his visit in 1920–21. "A Georgian uprising in favour of the restoration of large-scale land owner-ship is out of the question in Georgia," he wrote. "Most of the Georgian landed gentry, poor and indebted, had been forced to live off their labour, not their landed property, even before the revolution."

The landed gentry was not then, nor would it be a problem. "They have nothing to hope for from the return of the old conditions, but much to hope for from the economic prosperity of the country, which is possi-ble only under democratic forms." As for the rural working class, Kautsky wrote that "the vast majority of the peasantry in Georgia, like the wage-earners, is in the Menshevik camp."

During the Russian Civil War, the Georgians felt as threatened as the Bolsheviks did by the "uprisings of Kolchak, Denikin, [and] Wrangel," Kautsky wrote. They were also not keen to embrace the British and French imperialists, whom Kautsky described as the backers of the Russian White Guards and as threats to Georgian independence.

Before February 1921, the relationship between the Bolshevik gov-ernment in Moscow and independent Georgia was described by Kautsky as "quite tolerable, at times even friendly" despite the vast differences between the Bolsheviks and the Georgian Social Democrats. But the moment the Russian Civil War was over, he wrote, the Soviets "jumped at the throat of little Georgia with a single leap in order to throw her down and gag her."

The Georgian Social Democrats had refrained from attacking the Russians so long as there was a White Guard threat. Once that threat had disappeared in 1921, there began "intermittent Menshevik uprisings in Georgia against the Moscow regime."

Kautsky emphasized that uprisings like the Georgian one were not what Socialists wanted. The outcome of such uprisings was uncertain, he wrote. "Devastation and suffering" would be "immense." Socialists cer-tainly would prefer alternatives to civil war. But the goal remained the same: to get the Bolsheviks "to abandon or at least to alleviate their means of oppression."

Kautsky's book ends on an optimistic note. "Under no circumstances must the proletariat of Russia despair," he wrote. The problem is the "apa-thy and hopelessness of so many" Russian workers. This was undoubt-edly true in Georgia following the crushing of the 1924 uprising. "If it is possible to instil hope and interest" among those proletarians, Kautsky concluded, "the Bolshevik tyranny will soon crack at the seams."

As we know, this is not what happened. The "apathy and hopelessness" only grew in Soviet Russia and its colonies. The Bolshevik tyranny grew far more violent and oppressive and managed to survive for another two-thirds of a century.

But one thing did change: the attitude of the Socialists toward the Soviet regime. The Communists were no longer comrades who had gone astray. They were no longer a movement that Socialists should reach out to, seeking points of agreement. The hopes raised by Friedrich Adler at the 1922 Berlin meeting were now a distant memory—a memory of something that would never happen.

The old Socialist movement was finished. The new one was now ready to be born.

Conclusion

THE GEORGIAN NATIONAL UPRISING IN AUGUST 1924 left behind many unanswered questions. In this chapter, I'll try to answer some of these. It was a complex event with many different interpretations, including a remarkably honest evaluation by the Georgian Social Democratic leader, Noe Zhordania, which will be explored here. And finally, while it was an end to some things, it was also a new beginning for others—and I'll explain what I mean.

Let's start with some of the unanswered questions.

Why did the Cheka have such success infiltrating the underground opposition in the country?

During the years of Georgian independence, the Social Democratic government had its own counter-intelligence service which had considerable success in its fight against the local Bolsheviks.

But with the successful Red Army invasion in 1921, the flight of the Georgian government, and the defeat of the early armed uprisings, the tide had turned. The Cheka could now employ all the power of the Soviet state to pay informers, arrest those suspected of disloyalty, and so on. The Cheka's years of experience crushing the opposition inside Soviet Russia certainly helped.

The insurgents would be walking into a trap, as so much was already known of their plans. As Amy Knight wrote, "It seems that Beria and his superior, Kvantaliani, actually encouraged the rebellion so they would have a pretext for destroying all political opposition."[1]

The Soviet counter-insurgency strategy was largely intelligence-driven, and at its head was the newly appointed deputy head of the republic's Cheka, Lavrenty Beria. Beria went on to become head of Georgia's secret police, then the leader of its Communist Party, and was later brought to Moscow by Stalin to head up the secret police of the whole USSR. But it was in crushing the Georgian rebellion of 1924 that Beria proved his credentials.

Why did the uprising take place at all?

The Soviet historians were not entirely wrong when they claimed that the Georgians had been planning an armed insurrection for some time. There were many different ways to resist the Bolsheviks, peaceful and violent, and armed struggle was inevitably going to be one of the ways of fighting the dictatorship.

Preparation for the uprising included the formation of the Damkom and its military committee. With the arrest of that committee in 1923 and the execution of its members, it should have been clear that the Cheka had sources of information inside the resistance. And while that delayed the planned launch of the uprising, it did not prevent it.

This was never intended to be a spontaneous outbreak of violence. Like the Bolshevik seizure of power in Petrograd in 1917, this was supposed to be a planned and coordinated attack on the government, which would result in its losing control of the country, even if only temporarily. The Georgian rebels hoped that, given time, uprisings in neighboring countries would take place, and perhaps foreign military intervention as well. There was hope that the new Labour government in Britain, headed up by Ramsay MacDonald, who was then thought to be a friend of Georgia, might provide some military support. The Damkom leaders did not fully understand the international situation—but the government-in-exile did.

From 1921, there was concern, especially in the government-in-exile, that recognition and trade deals with the Soviets were imminent, especially in Britain. The window of opportunity for this kind of uprising was rapidly closing and soon there would be no possibility of help from the outside world.

The problem for the resistance was that by August 1924, it was clear that the Cheka knew a lot—not everything, but a lot—about the plans for the uprising. The leadership of the resistance had been decapitated in 1923 with the arrest of the Damkom's Military Committee, and even more so the following year with the capture of the Social Democratic leaders who had returned to Georgia, Khomeriki and Jugheli. The anti–Soviet forces had lost the element of surprise completely. And as we shall see, they were losing the ability to coordinate actions across the country.

As one Communist leader described it, despite the arrests of so many of the resistance leaders, the rebellion went ahead "as if under a kind of inertia."[2]

It was as if the Cheka *wanted* this to happen to bring the rebel fighters out of hiding and exterminate them, which is precisely what happened. An argument can be made that the uprising was a trap laid by Beria and the Cheka to destroy the Georgian Social Democrats and their allies.

Why did the insurgents in Chiatura jump the gun, starting the insurrection a day earlier than planned?

This completely gave away any element of surprise and allowed the Soviet regime to quickly suppress the rebellion in that part of the country.

One story we have reported is that the rebels in Chiatura heard the sound of gunfire and thought the insurrection had begun, so they started shooting too.

Others explain that the fighters in Chiatura did not jump the gun at all and that they rose up on the right date, which was timed to coincide with a religious holiday. They assumed that the Soviet forces would be drunk and easily overpowered. But if that were the case, why did their comrades in other parts of the country then wait a day to join them?

It's important to remember that communication between the various rebel groups was limited to begin with and they had to do all their planning and coordination secretly. We may never know why the insurrection started when it did.

Who betrayed the insurgents?

After his arrest, Jugheli became convinced that the Cheka knew all about the planned uprising including the date it was due to begin. The Cheka may have had several sources of information inside the ranks of the opposition, both in Georgia and abroad. The allegation that it was National Democrats inspired by their hatred of the Social Democrats is seemingly strengthened by Beria's "admission" in 1930 that the information came from them. But we have to keep in mind that it was in Beria's interest to divide the various non–Communist parties, which already distrusted each other.

Why did the Bolsheviks panic during and after the 1924 uprising in Georgia?

We have already discussed the panicked reaction of Soviet leaders, including Orjonikidze and Stalin, to an insurrection that, in hindsight, seemed to pose little threat to the Soviet regime in Georgia or the newly-created USSR. Both the bloody overreaction to the uprising and

Stalin's comparing it to the Kronstadt and Tambov rebellions indicate that the fear was genuine.

Perhaps the Communists understood how their policies made them deeply unpopular in the country. These included banning political parties, bringing the trade unions and cooperatives under state control, jailing, torturing, and murdering their political opponents, making life harder for the peasants, putting an end to Georgian national independence, and declaring war on the church. And the same was happening across all the republics of the newly formed Soviet Union.

And finally, how many people died in the uprising and its aftermath?

The short answer is that we don't know, and we may never know. The Soviets admitted to very few and got Clara Zetkin to claim that "only" 320 died. Some Soviet estimates put the number at 800. As Timothy Blauvelt learned from Georgian archivists, the number is 832.[3]

Most other estimates are significantly higher. Even the distinguished members of the British trade union delegation, which accepted the Soviet explanations for everything and refused to talk with their Georgian colleagues in the independent trade unions, accepted that 3,000 had died. They were told by their Communist hosts that most of those fell in combat and were not executed after the fighting, and they accepted that explanation.

In debates in the British Parliament in 1924, the number of 9,000 deaths was raised by an opposition MP, but dismissed by the Labour Party then leading the country as an exaggeration. Amy Knight in her biography of Beria puts the number even higher, possibly as many as 10,000 killed. And finally, we have the rather precise figure cited by Markus Wehnre of 12,578 people shot between August 29 and September 5, 1924.[4]

For nearly seven decades after the 1924 uprising, the only official version of the story in Georgia was the one offered up by Soviet historians.

For the most part, the Soviet historians ignored the uprising, offering only brief accounts of what happened. Despite the fears expressed by Stalin, Orjonikidze, and Zinoviev at the time, they eventually downplayed the significance of the threat.

The insurrection, they insisted, was a small matter, basically gangs of bandits, backed by foreign imperialists and the Social Democrats, with no popular support and easily suppressed.

But there is another interpretation of the uprising, and a radically different one—the view of the Georgian Social Democrats and particularly their leader, Noe Zhordania. In a short book entitled *What Happened?* published in Paris in 1925, Zhordania played the role of historian, looking back at the uprising that had taken place the previous year.

The Georgian leader began by explaining that all uprisings have both an organizational and military character, and the 1924 insurrection was no different. But he identified what he believed to be a unique characteristic of the Georgian uprising: it broke out in many different places, having been organized secretly, and from the outset involved very large numbers of people. "It is both an uprising and a revolution at the same time," he wrote. "Here the political organization and the nation merged."

He explained this successful mobilization as being a result of Bolshevik tyranny, contrasting the new Communist rulers with the previous tsarist ones. The tsarist rulers, he claimed, had more contact with the people than did their Communist successors. As a result, "the people at once and suddenly stood up, captured the communists and declared their power," he wrote.

Zhordania believed that there was "no connection at all between the people" and the Soviet regime, a view confirmed in part by Stalin's comments a few months earlier. Zhordania wrote about the complacency of the Communist rulers of occupied Georgia. Months before the uprising, in May 1924, he found an official report that declared that "forces such as the Menshevik Party, the National Democrats and the Young Marxists have completely or almost completely disappeared from the camp of our opponents."

Reports of the demise of the opposition parties proved to be somewhat exaggerated.

In Zhordania's view, the Communists had almost no support among the Georgian people. The Georgians were by and large loyal to those parties who had been ousted by the Soviet regime and declared illegal. The Georgian people, he wrote, "want independence." The people "raised the national and democratic flag, which had hung over Georgia for 3 years and was artificially torn down. The fact is that it is stored in the hearts of the people and from there no one can erase it."

Zhordania summarized what he called the "positive side of the uprising" by saying that the "Georgians publicly raised the issue of Georgia in the world. Both the enemy and the friend must be convinced that we want freedom." Because of the uprising's success in putting Georgia "on the practical political agenda of the world," the Bolsheviks were doing all they could to minimize its significance—having labeled it "an adventure."

But Zhordania was also aware that many Georgians turned against the uprising after its defeat. Defeat, he wrote, is not a sufficient reason to denounce a revolt. He cited several defeated insurrections that deserved praise, including the Paris workers' uprisings in 1848 and 1871, the December 1905 uprising in Moscow, and the Kronstadt mutiny in 1921.

To Zhordania, what matters was not so much whether the uprisings succeeded, as their purpose and ideology. The Paris Commune of 1871 is condemned by the Right and praised by the Socialists while the November 1917 coup in Russia is praised by the Bolsheviks and condemned by the Socialists. The important thing is the goal of the uprising—what it aimed to achieve. But he acknowledged that is important to achieve those goals while limiting the sacrifice. "Even planned things," he wrote, "in practice often do not come out well."

Rebellions, like wars, can end badly. Zhordania wrote that obviously, one wants to plan an uprising for the most favorable conditions. But sometimes reality becomes "unbearable," he noted. "The more unbearable the reality, the more people are in a hurry. That is why Marx says: it is not the people who start the uprising, but those who stand on the necks of the people."

The Georgian people had already suffered under the Bolsheviks for more than three years by August 1924. They could no longer bear it, he wrote. "We cannot blame Georgia for this," he concluded. "The culprits are only the Bolsheviks."

Zhordania then discussed some of the main problems with the 1924 uprising. First, he wrote, "No armed uprising took place in its centre, but rather unarmed people took to the streets here. That is, the uprising turned into a revolutionary movement. This weakened the uprising. Uprising and revolution are two different events and have different paths."

"There were mostly unarmed people in the West," he wrote. "In the east, armed detachments operated, but due to their small numbers could not resist the enemy."

The district of Svaneti, he wrote, "does not believe in unarmed fighting at all. Military detachments are really fighting here. The Svans were the last to surrender to the enemy in September."

Zhordania pointed out that another problem with the uprising was that it did not include an attack on "the main camp of the enemy"—and specifically named Tiflis and Batumi, which he called "the biggest strategic points."

Zhordania noted that "the uprising was to begin with the capture of Tiflis, which would suddenly create a revolutionary situation and lead to an uprising throughout Georgia, possibly involving the peoples of Azerbaijan and the mountains." This did not happen; there was no revolution across the Transcaucasian region.

Despite the clear military defeat of the uprising, Zhordania discovered a silver lining: the insurgents had won a moral victory. The uprising could be described, he wrote, as a "putsch" and he even compared it to the December 1924 failed Communist uprising in Reval (Tallinn), the capital of Estonia.

However, according to the Georgian leader, the Social Democrats managed to rally masses of people in support of the rebellion which gave it "a popular character." It was not a putsch. Zhordania explained that "from a military point of view this negative event became a positive event … and ensured the moral victory of the nation."

As a result, he wrote, Bolshevik propaganda proved ineffectual, and "no one in Europe believed them anymore." Zhordania summed up the uprising as a "physical defeat and moral victory."

Looking to the future, Zhordania was concerned about some Georgian Social Democrats beginning to accept the permanence of Soviet rule. He argued that while the military preparations for the uprising were not adequate, politically the uprising was absolutely right. His opponents argued that "since the uprising was defeated, we must believe in Moscow's domination." He described this view as "nonsense." "There are many ways to liberate a nation, and if one does not work, we must try the other," he wrote.

Though the uprising that began on August 28 would never be repeated, Zhordania did not rule out armed uprisings in the future. He stressed the importance of the isolation of the Soviet regime on the world stage. Georgia did not stand alone, he wrote. Even "the Russian people themselves want to defeat" the Communist regime. He expected that the Soviet regime would never be stable and would remain in such a state "until its death."

This proved to be over-optimistic.

The defeat of the uprising marked the end of Georgian independence for nearly 70 years. For Georgia and the Georgians, the 1924 uprising—even more than the Soviet invasion of 1921—meant the end of their independence. There was never another uprising on this scale.

But as we have seen, it was also the beginning of the great split on the Left between Democratic Socialists and Communists and led to the ultimate triumph of the ideas of Karl Kautsky, the first great Socialist critic of Lenin and his regime.

It was an end and a beginning too.

Epilogue:
Frankfurt, 1951

IN 1951, DELEGATES REPRESENTING SOCIAL DEMOCRATIC and Labor parties from around the world met in the ruins of a once-great European city, Frankfurt, to re-found the Second International. That International, created initially in Paris on the centenary of the French Revolution in 1889, had collapsed during the First World War and fell dormant during the Second.

With the war's end in 1945, efforts began to make one more attempt to create a federation of parties that aspired to the same goal—a goal that now had a new name: *democratic* socialism.

At a conference in Paris in December 1949, the French Socialists proposed that a manifesto be drawn up to explain the parties' shared vision to a new generation. According to Julius Braunthal, who was to become the general secretary of the new body, it was "the collective work of all member parties.... There is no other document in the history of the International which was the fruit of so much intensive collective work by individual parties. Never before had any resolution or manifesto been submitted to the parties for previous discussion." That discussion lasted a whole year and a half, producing four drafts.[1]

The process was radically different from anything that had come before it. The modern Socialist movement had as its foundational document a short pamphlet written by Karl Marx and Friedrich Engels a century earlier. The Communist Manifesto laid out the views of a tiny and unknown organization, the Communist League. Despite that, the Manifesto was translated into many languages, millions of copies were printed, and it remains in print even today.

The difference between the two manifestos was striking: the one was the work of two brilliant men, expressing ideas far ahead of their time, imagining a global labor movement that had yet to be born. The other was the collective vision of that movement after a century of struggle, triumphs, and disappointments.

Until 1951, none of the Internationals "had proclaimed the fundamental ideas on which they were based and the objectives they were trying to achieve," wrote Braunthal. This was certainly true of the Second International in all its various incarnations.[2]

The Frankfurt Congress in 1951 represented a new beginning for the Social Democratic and Labor parties. Those parties had decided together to define what they stood for at a time when "socialism" conjured up images of the Soviet Union in the minds of many people.

In addition to Social Democratic parties from across Europe—among them parties in exile from countries now under Communist rule—there were parties from India, Japan, and Uruguay. Canada was represented by the Cooperative Commonwealth Federation, the forerunner of today's New Democratic Party. There were also delegates from what remained of the Socialist Party in the United States, which was then in the final stages of its terminal decline.

The Communists predictably denounced the Frankfurt congress. They called it "a gathering of hardened Wall Street agents ... traitors and accomplices of the warmongers, intimately linked with the general staffs, intelligence services and ruling cliques of the capitalist countries."[3] Nothing had changed in their tone since Karl Radek denounced the Social Democrats at the Berlin meeting in 1922.

The Communists had good reason to detest and fear the new International, created at the beginning of the Cold War. The Communists were concerned—and rightly so—that the new International would challenge them with an alternative vision of socialism and would reject the Soviet claim that they had created the world's first "workers' state."

Many of those who had initially developed the idea of "democratic socialism" in the 1920s and 1930s were long gone, including Karl Kautsky, who had died in 1938.

A new generation met in Frankfurt to reconstitute the International and to define its goals. The declaration that they adopted was entitled "Aims and Tasks of Democratic Socialism," and the use of the adjective "democratic" was deliberate. It indicated how far the Social Democratic and Labor parties had come in the previous three decades.[4]

The new declaration repeated many of Kautsky's formulations word for word. It took a very firm position on the subject of Communism.

Founding meeting of the Socialist International, Frankfurt 1951 (used by permission, AdsD der FES, 6/FOTA031038).

Braunthal noted something important here. He wrote that "it was those parties which, in memoranda and during the debate, acknowledged their own basis in the Marxist tradition which demanded that the declaration should condemn Communism and its claim to derive its moral justification from Marxism."[5]

In Frankfurt in 1951, as Braunthal explained, the Social Democratic and Labor parties said their "final word on the question which had so deeply disturbed the Socialist movement from the beginning of the Bolshevik Revolution in Russia to the outbreak of the Second World War: the question whether a Socialist reorganization of society was possible only on a foundation of democracy, or whether it necessitated the establishment of a system of dictatorship."[6]

The declaration could not have been more straightforward. "Communism falsely claims a share in the Socialist tradition," it read. "In fact, it has distorted that tradition beyond recognition. It has built up a rigid theology which is incompatible with the critical spirit of Marxism."

"International Communism," the declaration continued, "is the instrument of a new imperialism. Wherever it has achieved power, it has destroyed freedom or the chance of gaining freedom. It is based on a militarist bureaucracy and a terrorist police. By producing glaring contrasts of wealth and privilege, it has created a new class society. Forced labour plays an important part in its economic organisation."

In a paragraph that could have been taken directly from Kautsky's writings three decades earlier, it said: "Without freedom there can be no Socialism. Socialism can be achieved only through democracy. Democracy can be fully realised only through Socialism."

Those three short sentences summarize Democratic Socialism. What were Democratic Socialists to do in a world where millions lived under Communist rule? According to the declaration, "Socialists express their solidarity with all peoples suffering under dictatorship, whether Fascist or Communist, in their efforts to win freedom."

That phrase—"whether Fascist or Communist"—the easy comparison between different types of totalitarian societies, has its roots in the early 1920s. At that time, some Socialists (including the Georgians) began to speak of the Soviet Communists as being no better than "red fascists." It echoes Karl Kautsky's view from 1924 that just as Socialists would support a rebellion against fascist rule in Italy, they should support opposition to authoritarian rule in the Soviet Union.

The Frankfurt Declaration announced clearly that Socialists "oppose totalitarianism in every form because it outrages human dignity." The word "totalitarianism" may have been a relatively new one in 1951, but the ideas behind it, like the ideas behind "democratic socialism," had their origins in the first years of the Communist-Socialist split.

Soon after its adoption, the Frankfurt Declaration was tested in practice.

Barely eight years after the end of the Second World War, and with much of Berlin in ruins, workers in the Soviet Zone rose up against Communist rule. The trigger was an increase in the demands for productivity—what might today be called "speed-up"—by the ruling Communist Party. What had initially begun as an industrial action, which was itself unusual in a totalitarian state, quickly evolved into a revolution with demands that the government resign, political prisoners be freed, free elections held, and Soviet troops withdrawn. What started as a walk-out by construction workers in East Berlin quickly spread across all of East Germany.

The uprising was initially quite successful. Panicked Communist officials fled their offices, which were ransacked by angry protestors, and jails were opened to release prisoners. But the uprising lasted for barely a day. What the local Communists could not do on their own, they could do with Soviet help. Soviet troops and tanks, which had so recently liberated Germany from the nightmare of Nazi rule, were used to impose a new totalitarian regime that remained in place for another 36 years.

The East German rebellion was swiftly suppressed like the Georgian uprising had been thirty years earlier. A month later, the Socialist International's Congress opened in Stockholm, and it had this to say about those East German workers: "They dared to rise against a totalitarian régime. They demonstrated before the whole world that the urge for liberty cannot be repressed. They gave a magnificent example to all the peoples in all countries under despotic domination."[7]

Much had changed since 1924, when the French Socialists and the British Labour Party failed to show solidarity with the Georgians, abandoning them to Soviet rule. By 1953, the Social Democratic and Labor parties had chosen sides in the Cold War. They opposed totalitarianism and supported democracy. There was no going back to attempts to reconcile the newly branded "Democratic Socialists" with the rulers of the vast Soviet empire. A conference like the one held in Berlin in 1922 had become unimaginable.

In practical terms, this meant support throughout the Socialist International for collective security, including institutions like NATO, founded with the full support of the British Labour Party and other Social Democratic parties across Europe.

That support continues up to the present day. Indeed, the Secretary General of NATO during the first part of Russia's war on Ukraine, Jens Stoltenberg, is a former leader of the Norwegian Labor Party—one of the founding parties of the Socialist International in Frankfurt.

By 1951, the break between the Socialist and Communist movements was finally complete—thanks in no small part to the long-forgotten Georgian uprising of 1924.

Appendix: Fate of
the Principal Characters

OF THE COMMUNIST LEADERS MENTIONED in this book, nearly all fell victim to the same terror they had helped unleash on Georgia in 1924.

Lavrenty Pavlovich Beria received the "Order of the Red Banner" for his role in suppressing the 1924 uprising in Georgia. He was one of the most powerful figures in the Soviet Union when Stalin died in 1953. But in December of that year, he was arrested; tried on charges of treason, terrorism, and counter-revolutionary activity dating back more than three decades; and shot.

Nikolai Bukharin, who represented the Communist International at the Berlin meeting in 1922, was a victim of the purges and stood at the center of a show trial in Moscow. He was executed by firing squad in March 1938.

Solomon Mogilevsky, the head of the Cheka in Georgia at the time of the 1924 rebellion, died in a mysterious plane crash in 1925. There is some suspicion that the pilot, a young Georgian airman, crashed the plane deliberately. Another theory has been put forward that Beria and Stalin arranged for Mogilevsky's death for their own reasons.

Sergo Orjonikidze, who had been in charge of the Transcaucasian region at the time of the 1924 rebellion, died at the height of the Stalin Terror in February 1937. The cause of his death is not completely clear. The Soviet leadership announced that he died of natural causes (heart failure) but there are suspicions that he was shot.

Karl Radek, who provided outstanding service to the Soviet regime in his attacks on the Georgians and their allies, was also subject to a show trial in Moscow and sentenced to 10 years of penal labor. He was killed in a labor camp in 1939, apparently at the instigation of the NKVD.

Josef Stalin died peacefully on March 5, 1953, having been the effective ruler of the Soviet Union for three decades.

Of the other Comintern delegates to the 1922 meeting in Berlin, three died of natural causes. Alfred Rosmer was a leader of the French Communist Party who was expelled from its ranks in 1924. He lived until 1964. Sen Katayama, the Japanese Communist, died in Moscow in 1933, still loyal to the Stalin regime. Clara Zetkin also died that same year in the Soviet Union, having escaped Nazi Germany—and she, too, died of natural causes.

For those Georgians who opposed the Soviet regime, the ones who managed to escape abroad managed—in most cases—to die of natural causes, but those trapped in the country fell victim to the Cheka.

Ambrose, the Catholicos of the Georgian Orthodox Church, was finally released from prison in early 1926. His health broken, he died in 1927.

Kakutsa Cholokashvili managed to escape Georgia after the failure of the 1924 uprising and died in 1930 of tuberculosis in France. He was just 41 years old.

Valiko Jugheli, the former commander of the People's Guard, was executed by the Georgian Cheka during the 1924 uprising.

Noe Khomeriki, the architect of the agrarian reform that was the single greatest achievement of the short-lived Georgian Democratic Republic, was also shot by the Cheka in 1924.

Noe Zhordania, the leader of the Georgian Social Democrats and president of the first Georgian republic, died peacefully near Paris on January 11, 1953, after three decades in exile. He was 84 years old. His death was followed a few weeks later by that of Stalin.

Chapter Notes

Preface

1. Rayfield, *Edge of Empires*, 345. This text is sometimes translated as "Perhaps we did go a little far, but we couldn't help ourselves."
2. Kautsky, *Georgia*, 311.

Chapter 1

1. Martov, *World Bolshevism*, 113.
2. From *The Class Struggle*, Vol. III, No. 1, February 1919. Retrieved from https://www.marxists.org/archive/debs/works/1919/daypeople.htm.
3. Luxemburg, *The Russian Revolution*, 14.
4. *Ibid.*, 102.
5. *Ibid.*, 89.
6. *Ibid.*, 85.
7. *Ibid.*, 108.
8. *Ibid.*, 33.
9. *Ibid.*, 49.
10. *Ibid.*, 62.
11. *Ibid.*, 69.
12. Russell, *The Practice and Theory of Bolshevism*, 114.
13. *Ibid.*, 117–118.
14. *Ibid.*, 92.
15. *Ibid.*, 131.
16. Goldman, *My Disillusionment in Russia*, Preface to the first volume of the American edition.
17. Gompers and Walling, *Out of Their Own Mouths*, vi.
18. *Ibid.*, 239.
19. Esperantists are advocates of the use of the international auxiliary language Esperanto, which was created by L.L. Zamenhof in 1887. For a time, it was quite popular in both the Socialist and Communist movements. Stalin, who may have studied Esperanto as a jailed revolutionary in tsarist times, turned against the movement later in life, ordered its suppression in the Soviet Union, and had many of the most prominent Esperantists shot.
20. Karp, *George Orwell and Russia*, 9.
21. *Ibid.*, 8.

Chapter 2

1. Karl Marx, *A Contribution to the Critique of Political Economy* (Progress, 1977), Preface. Retrieved from https://www.marxists.org/archive/marx/works/1859/critique-pol-economy/preface.htm.
2. Kautsky, *Road to Power*, 4.
3. Donald, *Marxism and Revolution*, 247.
4. Kautsky's use of the term "feudalism" to describe tsarist Russia—which Lenin did as well—is probably not accurate. Marx himself described Russia as being "semi-Asiatic," meaning that, unlike feudalism in Europe, it had an all-powerful state that stood above classes—a precursor to the modern totalitarian state.
5. Donald, *Marxism and Revolution*, 232.
6. *Ibid.*, 235.
7. *Ibid.*
8. Geary, *Kautsky*, 78.
9. Kautsky, *Dictatorship*, xxxiii–xxxiv.
10. Donald, *Marxism and Revolution*, 235.
11. Karl Kautsky, *Karl Kautsky: Selected Political Writings*, ed. and trans. Patrick Goode (Macmillan, 1983), 97.

12. Donald, *Marxism and Revolution*, 237.
13. Kautsky, *Dictatorship*, xx.
14. *Ibid.*, xxxv.
15. Donald, *Marxism and Revolution*, 237.
16. *Ibid.*, 238.
17. *Ibid.*, 240.
18. *Ibid.*, 240–241.
19. *Ibid.*, 240.
20. *Ibid.*
21. Karl Radek, *Dictatorship and Communism*, trans. Patrick Lavin (The Marxian Educational Society, 1920).
22. Geary, *Kautsky*, 78.
23. Kautsky, *The Road to Power*, lxi.

Chapter 3

1. Leszek Kołakowski, "What Is Socialism?" http://savingcommunities.org/docs/Kołakowski.leszek/whatissocialism.html.
2. MacDonald, "A Socialist State," 64–66.
3. *Ibid.*
4. *Ibid.*
5. Mrs. Philip Snowden, "A Political Pilgrim in Europe," http://archive.org/stream/politicalpilgrim00snowuoft/politicalpilgrim00snowuoft_djvu.txt.
6. MacDonald, "A Socialist State."
7. *The Times*, October 14, 1920, 7.
8. *Ibid.*
9. "A Promising Russian Border State," *Manchester Guardian*, October 12, 1920, 8.
10. *Ibid.*
11. Kautsky, *Georgia*, 311.

Chapter 4

1. Vera Broido, *Lenin and the Mensheviks: The Persecution of Socialists Under Bolshevism* (Gower, 1987), 50.
2. János Berecz, *1956 Counter-Revolution in Hungary—Words and Weapons* (Akadémiai Kiadó, 1986), 179.

Chapter 5

1. This was the regional bureau of the Russian Communist Party (Bolsheviks) in the Caucasus, established in 1920 to prepare for the Soviet takeover to the three independent countries there: Georgia, Armenia and Azerbaijan.
2. Tucker, *Stalin*, 236–237.
3. *Ibid.*
4. *Ibid.*
5. Lang, *Modern History*, 238.
6. *Ibid.*
7. *Ibid.*
8. Tucker, *Stalin*, 240.
9. *Ibid.*, 237.
10. *Ibid.*, 237–238.
11. Suny, *Stalin*, 90.
12. Levine's earlier book, published in 1931, made no mention of Stalin's possible role as a tsarist police spy.
13. George F. Kennan, "The Historiography of the Early Political Career of Stalin," *Proceedings of the American Philosophical Society* 115, no. 3 (1971), 167.

Chapter 6

1. *The Second and Third Internationals*, 68.
2. The quote has been attributed to Plekhanov, Lenin, and Trotsky.
3. Philip Mendes, "The Rise and Fall of the Jewish Labor Bund," *Jewish Currents*, Autumn 2013. https://jewishcurrents.org/rise-fall-jewish-labor-bund.
4. Rayfield, 340.
5. Seven decades later, Gamsakhurdia's son Zviad would become the first president of newly independent Georgia.
6. Rayfield, *Edge of Empires*, 340.
7. Lewin, *Lenin's Last Struggle*, 44–45.
8. *Ibid.*
9. Blauvelt and Akhobadze, "Perspectives on the August 1924 Uprising in Georgia," 4.
10. Lewin, *Lenin's Last Struggle*, 48.
11. *Ibid.*
12. *Ibid.*, 56.
13. *Ibid.*
14. *Ibid.*, 58.
15. Lang, *A Modern History of Georgia*, 242.

16. *Ibid.*
17. *Ibid.*, 99.
18. Blauvelt and Akhobadze, "Perspectives on the August 1924 Uprising in Georgia," 5.

Chapter 7

1. Rayfield, *Edge of Empires*, 329.
2. Jones, "Soviet Power in Transcaucasia," 622.
3. Foreign Bureau of the Social-Democratic Labour Party of Georgia, *Documents of the Social-Democratic Labour Party of Georgia*, 30.
4. *Ibid.*, 8.
5. *Ibid.*, 8–9.
6. Georgian Social Democratic Party, *Resolutions*, 1925, 8.

Chapter 8

1. Spargo, *Marxian Socialism and Religion*, 126.
2. *Ibid.*, 128.
3. *Ibid.*, 154.
4. Sigmund Freud, *The Future of an Illusion* (Penguin, 2008), 62.
5. Lang, *A Modern History of Georgia*, 40.
6. The full text of the open letter is here: "Russia Annexes Georgia—Georgian Patriarch's Letter to the 1922 Genoa Conference," *The Canadian Journal of Orthodox Christianity,* Vol. III, No. 3, Fall 2008, 67. Translation and commentary by Dn. Lasha Tchantouridze, PhD. https://www.cjoc.ca/pdf/Vol-3-F-2%20Russia%20Annexes%20Georgia.pdf.
7. Buxton, *Transcaucasia*, 46.
8. Lang, *A Modern History of Georgia*, 241.
9. Rayfield, *Edge of Empires*, 341.
10. Kolarz, *Religion in the Soviet Union*, 100.
11. *Ibid.*
12. Lang, *A Modern History of Georgia*, 241.
13. Kolarz, *Religion in the Soviet Union*, 100.

Chapter 9

1. Jones, "Soviet Power in Transcaucasia," 625.
2. Resolutions 1925, 8.
3. *Ibid.*, 9.
4. The Museum of Repressed Writers, Tbilisi.
5. *Ibid.*
6. *Ibid.*
7. *Ibid.*
8. Jones, "Soviet Power in Transcaucasia," 626.
9. *Ibid.*, 627.

Chapter 10

1. *Ibid.*, 619.
2. Georgian Social Democratic Party, *Resolutions.* 1925, 9–10.
3. Rayfield, *Edge of Empires,* 341.

Chapter 11

1. Kautsky, *Georgia*, 289.
2. *Ibid.*, 287.
3. *Ibid.*, 289.
4. Blauvelt and Akhobadze, "Perspectives on the August 1924 Uprising in Georgia," 13.
5. Ph. I Rabinovich, "Soviet Regime in Georgia: A Reply to Victor Serwy," *International Co-Operative Bulletin*, November 1922.
6. *Ibid.*
7. *Ibid.*
8. *Ibid.*
9. *Ibid.*
10. *Ibid.*
11. *Ibid.*

Chapter 12

1. *The Second and Third Internationals,* 7.
2. *Ibid.*, 25.
3. *Ibid.*, 26.
4. *Ibid.*
5. *Ibid.*, 34–35.

6. *Ibid.*, 35.
7. *Ibid.*
8. *Ibid.*
9. Cited in Giorgi Chkadua, "The August 1924 Uprising: Plan, Outcome and Interpretation" (Georgian Foundation for Strategic and International Studies), https://gfsis.org.ge/files/library/pdf/The-August-1924-Uprising:-Plan,-Outcome,-Interpretation-3198.pdf.
10. *Ibid.*, 35.
11. *Ibid.*, 42.
12. *Ibid.*
13. *Ibid.*
14. *Ibid.*
15. *Ibid.*, 52–53.
16. *Ibid.*, 53.
17. *Ibid.*
18. *Ibid.*
19. In an online search for a definition of what-aboutism, nearly all the examples cited were from the latter half of the twentieth century, often referring to the Soviet Union. But as can be seen here, it was also in common use in the Communist movement as early as 1922.
20. *Ibid.*
21. *Ibid.*
22. *Ibid.*, 53–54.
23. *Ibid.*, 54.
24. *Ibid.*, 57.
25. *Ibid.*, 58.
26. *Ibid.*
27. *Ibid.*
28. *Ibid.*
29. *Ibid.*, 59.
30. *Ibid.*
31. *Ibid.*
32. *Ibid.*, 67–68.
33. *Ibid.*, 68.
34. *Ibid.*
35. *Ibid.*
36. *Ibid.*, 68–69.
37. *Ibid.*, 69.
38. *Ibid.*
39. *Ibid.*
40. *Ibid.*
41. *Ibid.*, 69–70.
42. *Ibid.*, 75.
43. *Ibid.*
44. *Ibid.*, 84.

Chapter 13

1. Trotsky, *Stalin*, 268.
2. Trifonov, "The Smashing of the Menshevik-Kulak Revolt in Georgia in 1924," 4.
3. Lang, *A Modern History of Georgia*, 239.
4. Georgian Social Democratic Party, *Resolutions*, 1925, 10.
5. Suny, *The Making of the Georgian Nation*, 221.
6. *Ibid.*
7. *Ibid.*
8. *Ibid.*, 222.
9. *Ibid.*
10. Bolshevik propaganda against Georgian Social-Democrats (Mensheviks), http://www.idfi.ge/archive/?cat=read_topic&lang=en&topic=152.
11. Suny, *The Making of the Georgian Nation*, 222.
12. *Ibid.*, 221.
13. Braunthal, *History of the International*, 87.
14. *Ibid.*, 88.

Chapter 14

1. Lang, *A Modern History of Georgia*, 236.
2. *Ibid.*
3. *Ibid.*, 237.
4. *Ibid.*
5. *Ibid.*, 238.
6. Rayfield, *Edge of Empires*, 340.
7. Trifonov, "The Smashing of the Menshevik-Kulak Revolt in Georgia in 1924," 5–6.
8. *Communist Takeover and Occupation of Georgia*, 13.
9. Rayfield, *Edge of Empires*, 342–343.
10. Ministry of Internal Affairs of Georgia, *The Archival Bulletin*, April 2008, 17. Retrieved from http://webarchive.national archives.gov.uk/20090316054834/http%3A//archive.security.gov.ge/saarqivo_moambe.pdf.
11. *Ibid.*

Chapter 15

1. Rayfield, *Edge of Empires*, 344.

2. Lang, *A Modern History of Georgia*, 240.
3. Wittlin, *Commissar*, 110–111.
4. *Ibid.*
5. Sharadze, 183. Cited in Chkadua, *The August 1924 Uprising*, 2.
6. Beria, *My Father*, 8.
7. *Ibid.*
8. *Ibid.*
9. Lev Lur'e i Leonid Maliarov, *Lavrentiĭ Beriia. Krovavyĭ pragmatik* (BkhV-Peterburg, 2015), 94.
10. Beria, *My Father*, 8.
11. Lur'e i Maliarov, *Lavrentiĭ Beriia*, 94.
12. *Ibid.*
13. Blauvelt and Akhobadze, "Perspectives on the August 1924 Uprising in Georgia," 8.

Chapter 16

1. Blauvelt and Akhobadze, "Perspectives on the August 1924 Uprising in Georgia," 10.
2. Trifonov, "The Smashing of the Menshevik-Kulak Revolt in Georgia in 1924," 14.
3. From cipher messages about the uprising in Georgia, G.K. Ordzhonikidze to I.V. Stalin (copies to M.V. Frunze and V.R. Menzhinsky), August 30, 1924.
4. Rayfield, *Edge of Empires*, 344.
5. Trifonov, "The Smashing of the Menshevik-Kulak Revolt in Georgia in 1924," 15.
6. *Ibid.*, 15.
7. *Ibid.*, 16.
8. *Ibid.*
9. Wittlin, *Commissar*, 112.
10. Morchiladze, *Character*, 206.

Chapter 17

1. *The New York Times*, September 1, 1924. The reference is to the Damkom and Prince Kote Andronikashvili.
2. Cipher messages, TsA of the FSB of the Russian Federation, F. 2. Op. 2. D. 682. L. 3–4. https://istmat.org/node/53762.
3. *Ibid.*

4. *Ibid.*
5. Trifonov, "The Smashing of the Menshevik-Kulak Revolt in Georgia in 1924," 17.
6. Blauvelt, *Clientelism and Nationality in an Early Soviet Fiefdom*, 203.
7. Blauvelt and Akhobadze, "Perspectives on the August 1924 Uprising in Georgia," 9.
8. Cipher messages.
9. Wittlin, *Commissar*, 113.
10. Trifonov, "The Smashing of the Menshevik-Kulak Revolt in Georgia in 1924," 14–15.
11. *Communist Takeover and Occupation of Georgia*, 15.
12. Kautsky, *The International and Soviet Russia*, 16.
13. *Ibid.*
14. *Ibid.*
15. *Ibid.*
16. Trifonov, "The Smashing of the Menshevik-Kulak Revolt in Georgia in 1924," 15.
17. Rayfield, *Edge of Empires*, 345.
18. Cipher messages.
19. *Ibid.*
20. Wittlin, *Commissar*, 112.
21. Trifonov, "The Smashing of the Menshevik-Kulak Revolt in Georgia in 1924," 17–18.
22. Sulkhanishvili, *My Memories*, 159.
23. Cipher messages.
24. Trifonov, "The Smashing of the Menshevik-Kulak Revolt in Georgia in 1924," 16.
25. From cipher messages about the uprising in Georgia, Secretary of the Transcaucasian Regional Committee of the R.C.P.(B.) A.F. Myasnikov to I.V. Stalin (copy to F.E. Dzerzhinsky). September 2, 1924, No. 170. https://istmat.org/node/53762.
26. Cited in Knight, *Beria*, 33.
27. *Ibid.*
28. *Ibid.*
29. *Ibid.*
30. Rayfield, *Edge of Empires*, 345.
31. Knight, *Beria*, 33.
32. Trifonov, "The Smashing of the Menshevik-Kulak Revolt in Georgia in 1924," 4.

Chapter 18

1. From cipher messages about the uprising in Georgia, G.K. Ordzhonikidze to I.V. Stalin (copies to M.V. Frunze and V.R. Menzhinsky), August 30, 1924, 85.
2. From cypher messages about the uprising in Georgia, G.K. Ordzhonikidze to I.V. Stalin (copies to M.V. Frunze and V.R. Menzhinsky), August 30, 1924, 85.
3. Chkadua, *The August 1924 Uprising*, 6–7.
4. *Communist Takeover and Occupation of Georgia.*
5. Trifonov, "The Smashing of the Menshevik-Kulak Revolt in Georgia in 1924," 14.
6. *Ibid.*, 19.
7. Trotsky, *Stalin*, 268.
8. Ruth Fischer, *Stalin and German Communism: A Study in the Origins of the State Party* (Geoffrey Cumberlege and Oxford University Press, 1948), 472.
9. Stalin, *The Party's Immediate Tasks in the Countryside*, Speech Delivered at a Conference of Secretaries of Rural Party Units, Called by the Central Committee of the R.C.P.(B.) October 22, 1924. https://www.marxist-s.org/reference/archive/stalin/works/1924/10/22.htm.
10. Carr, *Socialism in One Country*, Vol. I, 199.
11. *Ibid.*
12. Pipes, *Russia Under the Bolshevik Regime*, 376.
13. *Ibid.*, 375.
14. *Ibid.*, 376.
15. *Ibid.*
16. *Ibid.*

Chapter 19

1. Dr. Lasha Bakradze, "The Exuberant Life and Tragic Death of the Blue Horns," https://civil.ge/archives/244366.
2. Knight, *Beria*, 33–34.
3. "24 Are Executed for Georgia Revolt," *The New York Times*, September 10, 1924.
4. *Ibid.*
5. Rayfield, *Edge of Empires*, 345.

6. Morchiladze and Nasmyth, *Character in Georgia*, 206.
7. *Communist Takeover and Occupation of Georgia.*
8. *Ibid.*
9. Makharadze, *Beniamin (Benia) Chkhikvishvili 1880–1924*, 108–111.
10. From cipher messages about the uprising in Georgia, I.V. Stalin to the Transcaucasian Regional Party Committee, September 2, 1924.
11. Knight, *Beria,* 35.
12. Blauvelt and Akhobadze, "Perspectives on the August 1924 Uprising in Georgia," 17.

Chapter 20

1. Museum of Repressed Writers, Tbilisi.
2. Bakradze, "The Exuberant Life and Tragic Death of the Blue Horns."

Chapter 21

1. Suladze, 214. The original document can be found in the Georgian National Archives: Central Historical Archive, F. 2117, Desc. 1, Doc. 295.
2. Suladze, *Assassination of the First Prime-Minister of Georgia Noe Ramishvili*, 194.

Chapter 22

1. Benda, *The Treason of the Intellectuals*, 145.
2. Trifonov, "The Smashing of the Menshevik-Kulak Revolt in Georgia in 1924," 5.
3. Markus Wehner, "Le soulèvement géorgien de 1924 et la réaction des Bolsheviks," *Communisme*, nos. 42–44, 1995, 155–170.
4. Max Shachtman, "Clara Zetkin: Founder of International Women's Day," *The Militant*, July 22, 1933. Reprinted in *Solidarity*, https://www.workersliberty.org/story/2023-03-14/clara-zetkin-founder-international-womens-day. The Shachtman article was reprinted in 2023 as

a response to an article I had written that was critical of Zetkin's role as an apologist for the Bolshevik massacres in Georgia.

5. From the website of the United States Holocaust Memorial Museum, https://encyclopedia.ushmm.org/content/en/article/henri-barbusse.

6. David-Fox, *Showcasing the Great Experiment*, 231.

7. *Ibid.*

8. *Ibid.*

9. *Ibid.*

10. Kandelaki, *The Georgian Question before the Free World*, 46.

11. *Ibid.*

12. *Ibid.*

13. *Ibid.*, 47.

Chapter 23

1. Lang, *A Modern History of Georgia*, 236.

2. *Ibid.*, 244.

3. https://hansard.parliament.uk/Commons/1924-10-02/debates/cecd6f80-fe4d-4b86-b6b7-690b74985aa5/Georgia.

4. *Ibid.*

5. *Ibid.*

6. Guram Sharadze, *History of the Georgian Emigrant Journalism*, Vol. I, 181. Cited in Chkadua, *The August 1924 Uprising*, 2.

7. Liebich, *From the Other Shore*, 176. His source is a letter from the Russian Menshevik leader Pavel Axelrod to the Georgian Social Democrat Irakli Tsereteli.

8. Blauvelt and Akhobadze, "Perspectives on the August 1924 Uprising in Georgia," 11.

Chapter 24

1. Articles from the *Daily Herald* collected in Trades Union Congress delegation to Russia (press cuttings), Warwick Digital Collections. https://cdm21047.contentdm.oclc.org/digital/collection/russian/id/8709/rec/17.

2. Adler, *The Anglo-Russian Report*, xxi.

3. *Ibid.*, 12.

4. Trifonov, "The Smashing of the Menshevik-Kulak Revolt in Georgia in 1924," 5.

5. Statement by exiled Georgian trade union leaders with appendices relating to the Bolshevik suppression of the 1924 August Uprising in Georgia.

Chapter 25

1. Otto Rühle, *From the Bourgeois to the Proletarian Revolution*, 1924. https://www.marxists.org/archive/ruhle/1924/revolution.htm.

2. Otto Rühle, "The Struggle Against Fascism Begins with the Struggle Against Bolshevism," *Living Marxism*, Vol. 4, No. 8, 1939. https://www.marxists.org/archive/ruhle/1939/ruhle01.htm.

3. *Ibid.*

4. Luigi Fabbri, *The Preventive Counter-Revolution*, https://www.katesharpleylibrary.net/8pk1j9.

5. Voline, "Red Fascism," *Ce qu'il faut dire* (Brussels), July 1934. https://theanarchistlibrary.org/library/voline-red-fascism.

6. Foreign Bureau of the Social-Democratic Labour Party of Georgia, *Documents of the Social-Democratic Labour Party of Georgia*, 10.

7. Foreign Bureau of the Social-Democratic Labour Party of Georgia, *Documents of the Social-Democratic Labour Party of Georgia*, Letter from the CC of the SDLPG to the German working class, 33.

Chapter 26

1. Roobol, *Tsereteli*, 224.

2. *Ibid.*, 224–225.

3. *Ibid.*, 225.

4. Kautsky, *The International and Soviet Russia*.

Conclusion

1. Knight, *Beria*, 32.

2. Blauvelt and Akhobadze, "Perspectives on the August 1924 Uprising in Georgia," 14.

3. *Ibid.*, 18.

4. Markus Wehner, "Le soulévement géorgien de 1924 et la réaction des Bolsheviks," *Communisme*, nos. 42–44, 1995, 155–170.

Epilogue

1. Braunthal, *History of the International*, 200.

2. *Ibid.*, 199.

3. *Ibid.*, 206.

4. The Declaration is available online: https://www.socialistinternational.org/congresses/i-frankfurt/.

5. Braunthal, *History of the International*, 202.

6. *Ibid.*, 201.

7. *Ibid.*, 395.

Bibliography

Archives and Documents

Communist Takeover and Occupation of Georgia. Special report no. 6 of the Select Committee on Communist Aggression, House of Representatives. Washington, D.C.: Government Printing Office, 1955.

Foreign Bureau of the Social-Democratic Labour Party of Georgia. *Documents of the Social-Democratic Labour Party of Georgia.* London: Foreign Bureau of the Social-Democratic Labour Party of Georgia, 1925.

Georgian National Archives: Central Historical Archive, Tbilisi, Georgia.

Georgian Social Democratic Party. *Resolutions of the Third Secret Conference of the "Illegal" SDLP Held Last Summer in Georgia.* 1925.

The Second and Third Internationals and the Vienna Union: Official Report of the Conference Between the Executives, Held at the Reichstag, Berlin, on the 2nd of April 1922 and following days. London: The Labour Publishing Company, 1922. The full text is online at https://collections.mun.ca/digital/collection/radical/id/7880.

Stalin, J.V. *The Party's Immediate Tasks in the Countryside.* Speech Delivered at a Conference of Secretaries of Rural Party Units, Called by the Central Committee of the R.C.P.(B.), October 22, 1924. *Works,* Vol. 6, January–November, 1924, 315–326. Retrieved from https://www.marxists.org/reference/archive/stalin/works/1924/10/22.htm.

Articles

Bakradze, Lasha. "The Exuberant Life and Tragic Death of the Blue Horns." https://civil.ge/archives/244366.

Blauvelt, Timothy, and Ketevan Akhobadze. "Perspectives on the August 1924 Uprising in Georgia." *Caucasus Survey,* 2024, 1–24.

Chkadua, Giorgi. "The August 1924 Uprising: Plan, Outcome and Interpretation." Georgian Foundation for Strategic and International Studies. https://gfsis.org.ge/files/library/pdf/The-August-1924-Uprising:-Plan,-Outcome,-Interpretation-3198.pdf.

Jones, Stephen. "The Establishment of Soviet Power in Transcaucasia: The Case of Georgia 1921–1928." *Soviet Studies,* vol. 40, no. 4, Oct. 1988, 616–639.

MacDonald, Ramsay. "A Socialist State in the Caucasus." *The Nation,* October 16, 1920, 64–66.

Trifonov, I. Ia. "The smashing of the Menshevik-Kulak Revolt in Georgia in 1924." *Soviet Studies in History* 16, no. 2, Fall 1977, 3–31.

Wehner, Markus. "Le soulévement géorgien de 1924 et la réaction des Bolsheviks." *Communisme,* nos. 42–44, 1995, 155–170.

Books

Adler, Friedrich. *The Anglo-Russian Report. a Criticism of the Report of the British Trades Union Delegation to Russia Etc.* P.S. King & Son, 1925.

Avrich, Paul. *Kronstadt 1921.* Princeton University Press, 2014.

Barbusse, Henri. *Voici ce qu'on a fait de la Géorgie*. Ernest Flammarion, 1929. Available online at https://gallica.bnf.fr/ark:/12148/bpt6k113324c/f133.item.r=1924#.

Benda, Julien. *The Treason of the Intellectuals (La Trahison Des Clercs)*. Trans. Richard Aldington. W.W. Norton, 1969.

Beria, Sergo. *My Father: Inside Stalin's Kremlin*. Trans. Françoise Thom, English trans. Brian Pearce. Duckworth, 2001.

Blauvelt, Timothy K. *Clientelism and Nationality in an Early Soviet Fiefdom: The Trials of Nestor Lakoba*. Routledge, 2021.

Brant, Stefan. *The East German Rising—17th June 1953*. Thames and Hudson, 1955.

Braunthal, Julius. *History of the International*. Gollancz, 1967.

Buxton, Rev. Harold. *Transcaucasia*. The Faith Press, 1926.

Carr, Edward Hallett. *Socialism in One Country 1924-1926*. Macmillan, 1958.

David-Fox, Michael. *Showcasing the Great Experiment: Cultural Diplomacy and Western Visitors to the Soviet Union, 1921-1941*. Oxford University Press, 2012.

Donald, Moira. *Marxism and Revolution: Karl Kautsky and the Russian Marxists 1900-1924*. Yale University Press, 1993.

Geary, Dick. *Kautsky*. Manchester University Press, 1987.

Goldman, Emma. *My Disillusionment in Russia*. Doubleday, Page & Company, 1923. Available online at https://www.marxists.org/reference/archive/goldman/works/1920s/disillusionment/index.htm.

Gompers, Samuel, and William English Walling. *Out of Their Own Mouths: A Revelation and an Indictment of Sovietism*. E.P. Dutton, 1921.

Jones, Stephen Francis. *Socialism in Georgian Colors: The European Road to Social Democracy, 1883-1917*. Harvard University Press, 2005.

Jordania, Noe. *What Happened*. Paris, 1925.

Kandelaki, Constantin. *The Georgian Question Before the Free World (Acts, Documents, Evidence)*. Impr. de Navarre, 1953.

Karp, Masha. *George Orwell and Russia*. Bloomsbury Academic, 2023.

Kautsky, Karl. *The Dictatorship of the Proletariat*. National Labour Press, 1919.

Kautsky, Karl. *Georgia, a Social-Democratic Peasant Republic, Impressions and Observations*. Trans H.J. Stenning, rev. Kautsky. International Bookshops, 1921. Reprinted in a trilingual edition in 2018 by Friedrich-Ebert-Stiftung Georgia.

Kautsky, Karl. *Die Internationale und Sowjetrussland (The International and Soviet Russia)*. Verlag J.H.W. Dietz Nachfolger, 1925. Available online at https://www.digitale-sammlungen.de/de/view/bsb11128294?page=5.

Kautsky, Karl, and John H. Kautsky. *The Road to Power: Political Reflections on Growing into the Revolution*. Humanities Press, 1996.

Knight, Amy. *Beria: Stalin's First Lieutenant*. Princeton University Press, 1993.

Kolarz, Walter. *Religion in the Soviet Union*. Macmillan, 1961.

Lang, David Marshall. *A Modern History of Georgia*. Weidenfeld and Nicolson, 1962.

Lerner, Warren. *Karl Radek: The Last Internationalist*. Stanford University Press, 1970.

Lewin, Moshe. *Lenin's Last Struggle*. Trans. A.M. Sheridan Smith from the French. Faber, 1969.

Liebich, André. *From the Other Shore: Russian Social Democracy after 1921*. Harvard University Press, 1997.

Luxemburg, Rosa. *The Russian Revolution and Leninism or Marxism?* University of Michigan Press, 1961.

Makharadze, Irakli. *Beniamin (Benia) Chkhikvishvili 1880-1924*. Institute for Development of Freedom of Information (IDFI), 2020. Available online at https://idfi.ge/public/upload/Blogs/Benia%20Chkhikvishvili-min.pdf.

Mett, Ida, and M. Bookchin. *The Kronstadt Uprising*. Theory and Practice, 2017.

Morchiladze, Aka, and Peter Nasmyth. *Character in Georgia*. MTA Publications, 2023.

Pipes, Richard. *Russia Under the Bolshevik Regime, 1919-1924*. Fontana, 1995.

Radkey, O.H. *The Unknown Civil War in Soviet Russia: A Study of the Green Movement in the Tambov Region, 1920–1921.* Hoover Institution Press, 1976.

Rayfield, Donald. *Edge of Empires: A History of Georgia.* Reaktion Books, 2012.

Roobol, W.H. *Tsereteli: A Democrat in the Russian Revolution: A Political Biography.* Trans. Philip Hyams and Lynne Richards from the Dutch. Martinus Nijhoff, 1976.

Russell, Bertrand. *The Practice and Theory of Bolshevism.* Allen and Unwin, 1949.

Sharadze, Guram. *History of the Georgian Emigrant Journalism*, Volume I. Tbilisi, 2001.

Smith, Edward Ellis. *The Young Stalin: The Early Years of an Elusive Revolutionary.* Cassell, 1968.

Souvarine, Boris. *Stalin: A Critical Survey of Bolshevism.* Trans.] C.L.R. James. Secker and Warburg, 1939.

Spargo, John. *Marxian Socialism and Religion: A Study of the Relation of Marxian Theories to the Fundamental Principles of Religion.* B.W. Huebsch, 1915.

Suladze, Gela. *Assassination of the First Prime-Minister of Georgia Noe Ramishvili: A Bloody Secret Operation of the Soviet Special Services.* Tsigni+Eri, 2018.

Sulkhanishvili, Aleksandre. *My Memories 1922–1924.* n.p., 1981.

Suny, Ronald Grigor. *The Making of the Georgian Nation.* Indiana University Press, 1994.

Suny, Ronald Grigor. *Stalin: Passage to Revolution.* Princeton University Press, 2020.

Trotsky, Leon. *Stalin: An Appraisal of the Man and His Influence.* Ed. and trans. Charles Malamuth from the Russian. Hollis and Carter, 1947.

Tucker, Robert C. *Stalin as Revolutionary 1879–1929: A Study in History and Personality.* W.W. Norton, 1973.

Wittlin, Tadeusz. *Commissar: The Life and Death of Lavrenty Pavlovich Beria.* Angus and Robertson, 1973.

Zetkin, Clara. *Imefreiten Kaukasus* (*In the Liberated Caucasus*). Verlag Für Literatur Und Politik, 1926.

Index

Index

Jugheli, Valiko 75, 96, 105–108, 120, 129–130, 135–136, 138, 144, 163, 168–169, 182

Kakhiani, Mikheil 114, 121
Kandelaki, Constantin 144–145
Kartsivadze, Davit 133
Kartsivadze, Nikoloz 100
Katayama, Sen 71, 182
Kautsky, John 21
Kautsky, Karl 1, 12, 17–24, 27, 30, 40, 54–55, 64–65, 71, 78, 115, 144, 161–166, 174, 176, 178
Kekelia, Archil 129
Kekelidze, Poka 133
Kennan, George F. 42
Kerensky, Alexander 81
Khomeriki, Noe 29, 62, 105, 129, 131, 163, 168, 182
Kołakowski, Leszek 25
Kolchak, Alexander 165
Kopali, Davit 59
Kvernadze, Nikoloz 133

Labour and Socialist International (LSI) 161–166
Lakoba, Nestor 114
Landia, Aleksandre 131
Lanti, Eugene 15–16, 141
Lenin, V.I. 11, 21–23, 31–33, 37, 46–48, 62, 71, 74, 86, 93, 102, 116, 161–162
Levine, Isaac Don 42
Ley, Robert 51
Lloyd George, David 147
Luxemburg, Rosa 12–14, 74, 139

MacDonald, James Ramsay 26–29, 31, 71, 76–78, 80–81, 146–147, 151, 168
Makharadze, Filipp 38, 47, 88, 117, 121
Malinovsky, Roman 103
Marquet, Adrien 27, 149
Martov, Julius 11, 70–72, 81, 89
Martynov, Aleksandr Samoilovich 88–89
Marx, Karl 17, 28, 157, 172, 175
Mazniashvili, Giorgi 137–138
Mchedishvili, Ioseb 59
Mdivani, Budu 39, 46–48, 74
Menzhinsky, Vyacheslav 120
Mills, John Edmund 148
Mirianashvili, Razhden 63
Mogilevsky, Solomon 181
Mussolini, Benito 158

Nodia, Vasil "Vaso" 131, 136, 154

Orekhelashvili, M.D. 117, 121
Orjonikidze, Sergo 1, 32, 34, 36–37, 45–49, 59, 86, 93–94, 106–107, 110–111, 116–117, 120–122, 127, 136, 169–170, 181
Orlov, Alexander 41
Orwell, George 16
Owen, Robert 65

Paghava, Gogita 99, 131
peasants 61–63
Petrini, Alfonso 158
Pipia, Daniel 133
Pirveli, Bidzina 97
Ponsonby, Arthur 148
Purcell, A.A. 150–151
Putin, Vladimir 102

Radek, Karl 44, 67, 71, 74–76, 79–83, 162, 176, 181
Ramishvili, Isidore 38
Rebellion (1924): beginning 109–111; Bolshevik leaders panic 120–127; British and French response 146–149; British trade union delegation 150–154; international reaction 139–145; post-uprising repression 128–132; preparations 102–108; spread 112–119; writers under attack 133–134; Zhordania's view 170–173
Remonidze, Silibistro 59
Renaudel, Pierre 27, 149
Rosmer, Alfred 71, 182
Rühle, Otto 157–159
Russell, Bertrand 14
Russia, Soviet: Karl Kautsky's view 17–24; left critics 11–16; "Red fascism" 157–160

Sarajishvili, David 58
Savinkov, Boris 108
Serrati, Giacinto Menotti 71, 77–79
Serwy, Victor 66
Shachtman, Max 141
Sharashidze, David 144
Sharashidze, Kristine 93–94
Shaumian, Stepan 41
Shaw, Tom 26, 71–72
Snowden, Ethel 26–28
Social Democratic Party: Georgian suppression of 85–90

9 781476 698663